MIDGE'S IRISH

Emerging from a Restricted Existence through Love and Support

P. J. LAMB

CONTENTS

Acknowledgements...1

Introduction...3

Chapter 1. The Loud-Voiced Scraggily Young Man...5

Chapter 2: Sir Warren Fools the Staff on Two Different Wards.............................10

Chapter 3: Buy One, Get One Free..15

Chapter 4. Irish Warren?...19

Chapter 5: Heartbreak..23

Chapter 6: An Ornery Summer for Warren..30

Chapter 7: Turning Things Around?...36

Chapter 8: Big Plans Self Sabotaged?...44

Chapter 9: Unlikely Discharge – Will It Last?...49

Chapter 10: The "Revolving Door" Starts...58

Chapter 11: The Revolving Door Continues..70

Chapter 12: Just When You Think He Is Out For Good...78

Chapter 13: Struggling In Society...86

Chapter 14: A One Month Stay This Time – Or Longer?.......................................93

Chapter 15: Stuck...101

Chapter 16: Rolling With The Punches..110

Chapter 17: Institutionalized Again?..116

Chapter 18: Finally: A Light At The End Of The Tunnel?....................................122

Chapter 19: An Ethical Dilemma And A Surprise..127

Chapter 20: Taking Things Into His Own Hands...133

Chapter 21: A New Beginning and a New Name 141

 Chapter 22: Are Things Starting To Go Downhill? 150

Chapter 23: Rebounding 158

Chapter 24: A Slow Self- Destruction for Ernie..................................172

 Chapter 25: Starting Over..180

Chapter 26: New Year, New Optimism 187

Chapter 27: Can Ernie Sustain Success?...196

Chapter 28: A Downhill Spiral 205

Chapter 29: Life Like A See Saw..214

Chapter 30: The New Decade – Off to a Bad Start.............................222

Chapter 31: A New Adventure 229

Chapter 32: A Year In Denver..243

Chapter 33: Epilogue 253

About the Author:..256

Acknowledgements

Thanks to people who supported, encouraged, or gave advice to this work. This includes, in alphabetical order: Tara Bess, Marty Bolton, Marc Cooke, Mark Eichenbaum, Pam Lamb, Sandy Lee, Spencer McKenna, Jack O'Brien, Jeanna Orphanidys, Katie Orphanidys, Randy Proctor, Melissa Waters, and also Jesse Gibbs and all the staff at Book Baby.

Introduction

Some people in America have had bad breaks growing up because of poverty, racial discrimination, family abuse, or chronic physical diseases. This story describes the life of someone who spent most of his teenage years through his twenties growing up in a state mental hospital in New England from 1967 to 1979, and his subsequent adjustment to living in the "real world." The years covered are from the mid-1970s to the early 1990s. Names of many people and places are either disguised or vague. In fact, once the main character left the state hospital for good, he started identifying himself by his middle name.

For clinical employees and patients in state hospitals in the northeastern US, the mid-1970s saw the beginning of the age of deinstitutionalization, unlike the prior decade when there were some "guard vs prisoner" types of staff, and many older clinical employees who felt that if too many patients were discharged, they would lose their jobs. However, attitudes for many staff started changing when administrators noticed that treating patients in the least restrictive environment with proper support services (instead of "dumping" them in the community to save the state money) was more humane than locking patients away indefinitely. Some long-term patients couldn't wait to get out of the hospital; some were resigned to consider the state hospital as their home forever. Other wanted to rebel and "fight the power" to make life miserable for any staff denying them what they perceived to be their right to freedom.

The protagonist in this story was one of the latter characters – someone who wanted to have a "cool and slick" image in his own way through braggadocio and manipulation of people. He was described by many staff as "grandiose" in his speech and ideas, "pathetic," and even as a "throwaway" human being, despite the fact that he aspired to be a normally functioning adult.

There were times when he made suicide attempts out of frustration and one attempt resulted in some permanent physical damage. His goal was to stay out of the state hospital forever, and he eventually accomplished this goal through help from younger staff and by falling in love with a female patient. Even though he had an exasperating journey of "ups and downs" fighting the pitfalls of impulsiveness as well as self-destructive personality behaviors, he finally found peace of mind and the ability to cope with adversity through belief in himself and assistance from other people.

This book is dedicated to young adults who feel trapped in their lives in some way, shape, or form by mental difficulties.

Chapter 1:
THE LOUD-VOICED SCRAGGILY
YOUNG MAN

Greg James was feeling tired from all the orientation meetings during his first day on the job as a mental health professional at Northern New England State Hospital. At 2:30, with no more meetings on the horizon, he sauntered back to his office, located in a corridor about 25 yards away from the ward to which he was primarily assigned. He thought, "It's great to have a couple of relaxing hours to set up my first office and make this a cozy space the way I want." A few minutes later, just after he set his desk calendar to the week of December 8th 1975, and started to enter some scheduled meetings for the week, a fairly short, wiry-built, wide-eyed young man who was unkempt in appearance (scraggly hair and moustache, and mismatched old clothes) barged into his office and began to yell.

"I don't know who the hell you are, but we haven't had group therapy in almost three weeks and I haven't seen any therapist alone since before Thanksgiving. I want to get out of this place and get away from these damn nurses who hate me. So do your job!"

He started to turn and limp away, but Greg stood up and said, "Hey – come here. What's your name? I just started here today, and I haven't met any patients yet."

"Warren Le Blanc is my name. You can call me Sir Warren," the guy arrogantly stated.

"Gregory James is my name. You can call me Mr. James."

"So, you're not Dr. James?"

"Not yet. Maybe in a few years. But I'm not a student. I'm on the staff here."

"Did you ever work in this bughouse before?"

"No. I came from upstate New York."

"Good. I don't know you, and you don't know me. But I want to be in your group therapy before I can trust you. You better start group therapy this week."

Warren turned around and half walked, half limped away, as Greg called out, "I'll see what I can do, Warren."

About 20 minutes later, Greg went out to the ward and asked Cindy, the head nurse, "What's the story with Warren Le Blanc?"

"Be careful with that guy. He's bad news," Cindy replied.

"I'd like to take his chart to my office and read it."

"Sign out for it here on this card. Bring it back before you leave today."

Greg opened the thick chart and read what case history was there, as well as notes from about the last 6 months. Warren, who was 25, had been in the hospital for almost nine years. He grew up in an apparently cha-otic environment, shunted back and forth from parents to other relatives, and he spent most of his childhood and early teenage years living with his grandfather. He had an 8th grade education. Apparently, his grandfather could no longer take care of him due to Warren's rebelliousness and angry outbursts and fights with people on the street, so he was enrolled in a residential school for industrial training when he was 16. After a few months there, he started getting "atypical seizures," which were attributed to nightmares until he was observed having such a seizure during the daytime. The Superintendent of the school recommended that he be admitted to the state hospital as a "voluntary minor." Diagnoses on admission were, "Seizures, Etiology Unknown," and "Sociopathic Personality."

Warren had been put on various doses of Dilantin, Luminal, and also Thorazine IM prn (prn = "as needed") to control his seizures and occasional "aggressiveness, assaults, and resistance to treatment." After the first year, he had become consistently quiet and cooperative for several months and had attained a less restrictive level of privileges where he could roam around the hospital grounds freely. But after a few days with this freedom, in July, 1968, he escaped from the hospital, broke into a downtown department store, and spent the night there. Police found him, brought him back to the hospital, and he was put in the Maximum Security unit. For the next 18 months he became more obnoxious to people and rebellious to staff, including outrageous bragging about socially unacceptable events he claimed he performed, which led to getting into fights with other patients. In January, 1970, he swallowed three ounces of ammonia in a suicide attempt. He showed no improvement in his behavior, and in 1971 he escaped from the hospital again briefly. Police were called when he was discovered having a grand mal seizure downtown and he was returned to the hospital. At that time, his medications were Mysoline, Phenobarbital, and Mellaril. However, in the next year, his seizures seemed to be increasing and he began having many physical complaints, decreasing coordination, and "much attention seeking behavior."

Through 1973, his mental status and behavior began to improve steadily and he worked at the sheltered workshop on the hospital grounds.

However, that October, he was beaten up badly in a fight with another patient, sustaining a broken jaw. He was transferred to the Medical/Surgical Unit for two months. He lost much weight and the sheltered workshop would not take him back until his physical condition significantly improved. Soon after returning to his geographic unit, he kept making demands to staff that he needed to be transferred back to the Medical/Surgical unit because he still felt "weak," and claimed that "at least I was treated like a human being there." After a couple of weeks of his requests being denied, he made another suicide attempt by jumping out of a 4th floor window of his hospital unit's building, fracturing his right foot and ankle badly. He also sustained a severe compression fracture of his L-4 vertebra. This left him with a permanent slight limp. He was in a local hospital for about a week before being admitted back to the Medical/Surgical unit for several months. When he started improving physically there, he became angry, uncooperative, and he was sent to the Maximum Security unit for a few weeks before going back to his regular geographic unit in June.

Although he seemed to improve enough to have a patient payroll job at the hospital laundry by the end of 1974, he spent a couple of brief periods in the Maximum Security unit due to violent outbursts toward staff, which caused him to lose his job. One of these verbal outbursts was because he thought he was treated unfairly when he was sent to a new Behavior Modification ward of the unit. Grandiosity, hostile outbursts, somatic complaints, and uncooperativeness to staff continued intermittently through much of 1975. His hygiene was also becoming a problem. He started improving quite a bit in the fall, did well again at the same patient payroll job, and some staff thought he should be considered for discharge to a group home. But he got caught drinking at a downtown bar twice (the second time he claimed he wanted to drink himself to death) and in November he wrote a grandiose note threatening to blow up the building if his off grounds privileges were not restored. He was sent to the Maximum Security unit for a few days, but came back to his geographic unit just before Greg met him.

Greg closed the chart, brought it back to the ward, and went home. On his way out the door he thought, "I'll see if I can help this guy, but I sure can't do it alone. It's gonna be tough, but maybe he'll get a chance to make it out of here someday."

Chapter 2:

SIR WARREN FOOLS THE STAFF ON TWO DIFFERENT WARDS

Warren was transferred to the locked Behavior Modification ward of his hospital unit soon after Greg's first encounter with him. Greg's interactions with him became somewhat informal - about 10 to 15 minutes every week through the first week of January. In the team meetings, staff on the ward agreed with Greg that Warren seemed to be grudgingly compliant with the program, even though he expressed a dislike for patients not getting enough tokens for good behaviors or therapeutic accomplishments. However, Warren made a deal with ward staff to trade in the tokens for increased privileges instead of goods in the ward "store," which had many things you could get at the hospital Patio Shop – an on grounds patient hangout that included a snack bar. He was granted limited off grounds privileges for an hour a day, three days per week, and he got his part-time patient payroll job back at the hospital laundry.

During the second week of January, however, one of the patients complained to staff that Warren was "trading tokens for favors and selling tokens to us for a dime apiece, or three for a quarter." The staff soon realized that Warren seemed to have far more tokens than anyone else on the ward, and although his behavior was better, it did not seem to merit this wealth of tokens. Several days later, one of the aides on the ward cautiously stalked Warren one day when he went downtown. It was learned that Warren went into a store that sold cards, games, chips, etc., and bought 100 tokens – 50 red (a higher value on the ward's program) and 50 blue. As soon as Warren returned, they found about 150 tokens in his dresser, hidden in his socks. Warren suddenly got very angry, not so much for being caught, but for the whole behavior modification token economy system. He immediately verbally and physically started to attack the staff member who confronted him, and he was sent to the Maximum Security unit for the rest of the month. The unit staff had a morning-long team meeting the next day, and it was decided to phase in punch cards for gaining points instead of tokens, with the charge nurse for each shift controlling the punch cards. At the end of the next week, there were no more tokens on any of the hospital units where there were Behavior Modification wards.

A social worker, a foreign psychology student, and Greg started group therapy in January on an open ward that consisted of some recently admitted patients, some acute patients, and some chronic patients. Warren was a resident of this ward when he got out of maximum security, and in the team meeting the day after his return, Greg lobbied to include him in this group. In his first group session, because he and another patient were new to the group, all members introduced themselves in the first few minutes. Then came Warren's turn.

"I am Sir Warren Le Blanc. I already know more than half of you here. I need no more introduction," he said, haughtily (but smiling).

One patient said, "Will you cut out that 'Sir Warren' crap. You're about as much royalty as the cockroaches that come in my room."

Another patient chimed in, "Let him call himself that. I think it's funny. We laugh at him."

Nobody wanted to discuss this further. He briefly told his story about how he had been in the state hospital for years and almost proudly stated that he survived a suicide attempt ("I jumped off the top of this building and this bughouse still couldn't kill me!"). He tried to monopolize the group discussion for the next 10 minutes before he suddenly folded his arms, crossed his legs and declared, "That's all I have to say. But watch out for most of the nurses here, you new people."

He refused to come to the next session, saying to Greg that he was "sick – sick of this hospital and the older nurses here!" Later that day, Greg talked with him briefly and Warren told him, "I don't want to see you for any individual therapy sessions, but I promise I will come to the next group session."

The following Tuesday he came to the group dressed outlandishly – it was almost comical. He wore a Russian hat, sunglasses, a ragged scarf, a multi-colored checked shirt, a western vest that had a hole in it, pajama bottoms, and snow boots. When the group started, he pulled out a cigarette holder and lit up a hand-rolled cigarette stuffed into it. As soon as he did this, the group turned their attention to him. Some people laughed; a couple people grumbled about he was making an ass out of himself ("Par for the course with him," one patient said). Then the discussion turned to dressing like pimps and whores, and doing drugs.

Warren declared, "Oh, I smoke Acapulco Gold. I have some in my room, and if you don't believe me, I will smoke it tonight!" After some group members confronted him about this and a couple of other grandiosities he expressed, he insisted that he could control the ward more than the staff when he wanted to.

"That might be half true, as we have seen," the social worker remarked, "but is that helping you get out of the hospital and avoiding making enemies?"

"I will leave here on my own terms when the time comes and I will win the fight against staff here in the long run."

The graduate student brought up the observation of him trying to emulate Elton John with his outrageous dress and mannerisms because he possibly wanted power and adoration similar to that of Elton John's fans. Warren smiled and replied that he appreciated the compliment.

He continued, "That is why I am Sir Warren (Elton John would not be "Sir Elton" for another 12 years). And I even roll some funk of my own," as he puffed on another cigarette, blowing a smoke ring.

This evoked a lot of laughter – Warren even laughed (Elton John had just come out with a record called "Grow Some Funk of Your Own."). The group briefly discussed arrogant people and how they reacted to condescending remarks before the session ended.

Sure enough, that evening at 8 o'clock nursing staff detected the smell of marijuana coming from out of Warren's room. One older nurse stated elatedly, "Now we got him red-handed!" Several staff barged into his room, confiscated a pipe and got Warren transferred to the Maximum Security unit after discussing the situation with the psychiatrist on call. Warren was screaming that it wasn't fair, as he was escorted off the ward. The psychiatrist on call said to send the pipe and the substance Warren was smoking to the hospital lab ASAP.

The next day, after the lab determined whatever Warren was smoking was not cannabis at all, staff thoroughly searched his room and found four tea bags in a small container underneath some papers in his top drawer. It turned out that Warren was smoking Lipton tea – his version of Acapulco Gold! One of the aides, the next day outside on his break, lit up a pipe bowl with some tea in it and he said it tasted and smelled just like marijuana, but it burned hot in the bowl and he declared that there was no way anyone could get high from it.

Warren was transferred back to the open ward of his geographic unit immediately, and smiled as he passed the nurses' station, as some angry, embarrassed nurses sneered at him. He continued his passive-aggressive behavior toward staff over the next few weeks, and although he did not dress strangely when he came to group therapy, his grandiose statements about things he had done at the hospital and what he was able to do continued. At the end of March, he wrote a note to the head nurse about how he was going to burn down the building "to set everyone free," and he went back to Maximum Security for a week. When he returned, Warren was brought into team meeting and he agreed to see Greg for individual therapy sessions with a behavioral contract. However, when the contract was presented to him to sign, he initially complained, "This is your version of an April Fool's Day joke, and I'm not gonna fall for that."

Chapter 3:
BUY ONE, GET ONE FREE

Later in the week, Warren agreed to see Greg to discuss a behavioral contract with which Greg thought Warren might comply. Greg knew that Warren would never agree to any of the specifics unless Warren insisted on writing some of the contract himself. However, anything Warren suggested would probably be unacceptable to the majority of the staff. Therefore, Greg included elements in the contract that he thought would be essential toward Warren finally getting out of the hospital. The first thing Greg listed was a long-range goal – to participate in a patient payroll job three days a week at the hospital bookbindery. The second item was that Warren would, every day, present himself with acceptable hygiene and dress appropriate for the season of the year to the nurse or aide assigned to monitor him on the day shift. Third, he was to demonstrate weekly improvement in controlling his anger through a cognitive technique learned in therapy sessions with Greg that focused on anticipating consequences of maladaptive behaviors. Fourth, he was to attend his scheduled activities for the entire length of the sessions. Fifth, he would select a designated mental health worker on the ward to consult with if he had any problems with staff or the unit programs – or Greg, if Greg were available. Finally, Warren would go off grounds only if he were accompanied by a staff person. If Warren complied with the contract for one month, he would attain off grounds privileges alone.

When Warren read the contract, he threw it back at Greg, and shouted, "No! I refuse to sign this. I'm not going along with this stupid contract. It's worse than being back on the behavior mod ward. I am me! I am not one of these robots snowed on meds that the nurses drove crazier than when they came here."

Greg replied, "Warren, if you don't show improvement in your hygiene, your anger, and take responsibility for your behavior, you're never gonna get out of here. Dr. Dell is trying to get more people out of here who have been here for a long time, but if you continue to fight the system here with any kind of open anger, every nurse and most of the aides will be dead set against you leaving the hospital."

"Well, I'll tell you this because I think I trust you. I snuck out of here last Saturday and I went downtown to see 'One Flew Over The Cuckoo's Nest.' Randall McMurphy was a great man. I don't believe he ever really stole a boat, though. But that hospital in the movie is a lot like this place, at least when I first came here. And the things he did were some of the only ways to survive in the bughouse. That's all we are – bugs. I'm too smart for most people here. I got two choices – fight the powers here or kill myself so they'll be sorry and have it on their consciences, if they have any."

"You know, in the meantime, you get more and more miserable. Any so-called victories you have like smoking that Lipton tea last month don't last. Did anybody get fired for that? Did your life improve because of that stunt? Look how Randall McMurphy ended up in the movie. Good thing for you they don't do electroshock therapy here. So, let's start with you and I drawing up a schedule of activities that you'd feel comfortable with, including the patient payroll job part-time at the bookbindery. You really need to improve your hygiene and appearance consistently – I think you look good today, and you don't have any body odor. I'll give you feedback on your appearance every day I see you. Most of all about your anger: think before you act - before you say something that might start a fight. Tell yourself mentally to stop – think of what might get you sent to the time out room, seclusion (locked time out) or the Maximum Security unit. Danger to self or others are the things that keep people here for a long time."

"OK. It's a deal – for now. But it's not a written contract that I have to sign," he said, surprisingly.

"I'll see you a couple times a week later in the afternoons – we'll make it informal. Come back to my office anytime between 3 and 4 o'clock, and if I'm not with somebody and my door is open, c'mon in. I also want you to come to group therapy, if you're not working at the bookbindery. I'll bring up what we discussed in the team meeting tomorrow."

"You better not turn into one of them – like I'm a criminal and you're a cop."

"I'm not a cop. At best, it's 1/3 me trying to help, but it's 2/3 you for trying to seriously improve your life so you can make it out of here."

Over the next few weeks, Warren showed significant improvement. Gina (his social worker) and Greg lobbied hard to get him to go to his grandfather's home on a weekend pass in order to see how he would react to what little family he had and to re-acquaint him with life in a small town. Unfortunately, he constantly argued with his grandfather and he was brought back Easter Sunday morning. He was angry that his grandfather wouldn't keep him for at least a week. Over the next few days his hygiene started to slip a bit, and he had incidents of being verbally combative toward a couple of nurses. In one brief impulsive display of anger, he not only screamed at Gina for not trying to help him go to wherever his mother's house was for a visit instead of seeing his grandfather, but he also lifted up part of the heavy pool table in the corridor outside of the ward and slammed it down, shocking everyone in the immediate area.

At the end of the month, nurses, activity therapy staff, and several patients got together to have a bake sale. Warren wanted to participate, but they refused to include him, telling him bluntly that they could never trust him because he would sabotage the entire thing. Warren was angry at this rejection, and now he was determined to undermine this event.

On the morning of the bake sale, Warren sneaked off grounds several blocks away to a local store that had a small deli. He bought two pounds of ham, a pound of Swiss cheese, two loaves of sliced fresh Italian bread, and two 6-packs of soda. He trudged back to the hospital grounds, broke into the rear of another building that had been closed for several years, and he left these items in an empty room. Then he went back to his room on the unit, got a piece of white cardboard and a crayon, and went back to the next building. By this time, it was almost 11:30, and at noon the bake sale was starting out in front of the building where his unit was. But Warren was out in back of his unit's building, sitting along the narrow road with a sign: "Ham and Cheese Sandwiches $3 – BUY ONE, GET ONE FREE! Soda 20 Cents a Can! Exact change, please. Tips welcome."

By 12:15, word got around the hospital about the sandwiches, and staff in other buildings thought it was in addition to the bake sale by the unit. Warren's business was booming. Just as he sold out of the sandwiches and soda, someone complimented the staff out in front of the building about the lunch deal out back as part of the bake sale. Nurses were irate when they saw what Warren was doing. They put him back in his room with no privileges to go off the ward unless it was for individual or group therapy with Greg. In team meeting the next day, Dr. Dell agreed with nursing staff, and Warren was restricted to the ward for a week.

Warren made $35 on the deal – as much as staff made on the bake sale.

Chapter 4:
IRISH WARREN?

After a week of restriction, Warren again started to improve his behavior and was able to regain grounds privileges. However, even though he was prohibited from going off grounds, he found ways to sneak off when he needed to feel free and blend in with people downtown. He started hiding any money he earned, or otherwise accumulated, in a room in one of the abandoned buildings on grounds to keep it from being stolen. He insisted to Greg that he never stole anything from other people because, "I never needed to. I only make deals with others when I really have to." What did he do with his money? He ate at one of the cheap "greasy spoon" places downtown sometimes, or he bought various health products or food. In a therapy session in May, he told Greg all the reasons he could not eat many hospital food offerings.

"Plain milk alone upsets my stomach. I can't drink coffee or tea without milk or sugar, or I'll vomit. I can't drink tomato juice or I'll vomit.

Cooked tomatoes make me sick. Spaghetti and meatballs make me sick. America chop suey (elbow macaroni in meat sauce) makes me sick. Coconut makes me sick. Sausage and eggs together make me sick. Same for baked beans, brown bread, most soups, and creamed codfish or beef stew. Ensure is too sweet for my system. So are most desserts – most pies and cakes with frosting, and ice cream. Same thing for pancakes or French toast if maple syrup is on them. Jelly, too. Macaroni and cheese binds me up terrible. Most of the canned fruits and vegetables they have here give me diarrhea. I can only drink some diet sodas or water."

Greg said, "That doesn't leave much. No wonder you're so thin. What do you eat when you go downtown?"

"I can eat hot dogs. I can eat potato chips. I can eat ham, turkey, roast beef, or chicken. I can eat rice, or mashed potatoes, or French fries. I can eat toast. I can have a Hershey's Semi-Sweet candy bar. I can drink beer or brandy. Sometimes I bring stuff back to my hiding place. I got a zippered cooler and plastic bags I put some food in so the cockroaches won't get it. I don't store most foods for any more than a couple of days, though."

"You are a real survivor."

"There's a lot of other things I bought in the past week that I needed. An athletic supporter, two tubes of tiger balm, a Timberland gift set that has a wallet and ski hat, Nytol, Vaseline, Desenex, Ban deodorant, baby powder, Vitamin E, cod liver oil, Tylenol, and a bowl. I also bought a pint of apricot brandy and a 6-pack of beer. I had to make a few trips. I spent all the money I had selling sandwiches."

"The Nytol, Tylenol, brandy, and the beer are things I have to tell the staff about in team meeting tomorrow."

"I'll deny it if you do. They'll never find the stuff, anyway. I'm not gonna kill myself. I got a girlfriend now. I met her when I was walking on grounds last week, and we went to the Patio Shop for a while. She's a patient on a unit in the Main Building. Some of those things I bought are for her. Some of the stuff we're gonna share."

"Tell me about this girl."

He smiled and said, "Her name is Midge McSorley. She's an Irish girl, about my age. It's her third time here. I haven't had a girlfriend in a long, long time."

"I guess that's why you've seemed happier lately, and you're doing so much better lately. You're complying with your treatment plan and not getting into any fights with staff or patients, lately."

He grinned and said, "I hope we can get out of the bughouse together. She's hoping to leave next month. She told me she's not depressed any more since she met me."

In the team meeting the next morning, when Greg told staff some of the things from yesterday's session that they needed to know, several comments were made to the effect that Greg shouldn't believe what Warren said. Most of the staff dismissively said that Warren was just being grandiose again.

However, Dr. Dell, the unit psychiatrist, stated, "It's good that he has a girlfriend, if it's true. If he keeps up his good behavior, maybe we can get him out of here and into a group home in a few months. Apparently, he's doing well in the bookbindery, going to all of his activities, and his hygiene and appearance are better. He's taking his meds as prescribed."

One of the nurses declared, "He's still not making his bed and the nightstand in his room is always messy."

Greg retorted, "So is my bed and my nightstand at home."

Patti, the supervising nurse on the unit, said, "Shame on you, Greg. You didn't learn anything from the Army several years ago."

The meeting ended on this laughing note.

In the individual therapy session, a week later, Warren related that he hadn't been this happy in years. He said that over the weekend he dropped by Greg's house with Midge to visit, but, "You weren't home."

Greg surprisingly asked, "How do you know where I live?"

"The new phone book came out Friday and I saw that you only live a few blocks away from here. I decided to save a dime and just come over to your place so you could meet Midge."

A fairly long discussion followed about what is appropriate and what is not regarding therapeutic boundaries, and patient-therapist roles. Warren surprisingly showed no indication of anger, resentment, or feelings of rejection. As this segment of the session ended, Warren suddenly blurted out, "Midge is Irish. I want to be Irish. From now on, you and everyone else can call me 'Irish Warren.' Better yet, people can call me 'Midge's Irish.' That sounds good."

"If I owned a race horse, I'd name it Midge's Irish," Greg said. They both laughed.

Warren said, "Here – I have something to show you."

Warren had a small plastic bag and pulled out two small cardboard paintings. Both were of very young girls – one was presenting an ice cream cone; the other had a bandanna and a sheepish grin.

Warren said, "That's Midge. It's paint by the numbers I made in OT (Occupational Therapy) this afternoon. But I bet she looked something like this 10 or 15 years ago. I'm gonna give them to her tonight."

Has anybody else in our building seen this girl?"

"Only Bob Caulfield (a patient on the Behavior Modification ward in the building). I don't want any of these jerks around her if I can help it. I go and meet her outside of her building, or we get together somewhere on grounds."

"Well, it's good to see you happy most of the time now. Hopefully, we can get you out of this place sometime soon, if you can sustain your good behavior, and don't fall into self-destructiveness. Good luck with Midge, Warren."

"Don't call me Warren. Call me 'Irish.' Or 'Irish Warren.' Or, 'Midge's Irish.'"

HEARTBREAK

For the rest of May, Warren kept up his good behavior, being consistently cooperative with staff, and smiling more often. He was still following all the unit rules, going to all activities on his schedule, and doing well at the bookbindery. Much of his spare time was spent off the unit with Midge at various places on hospital grounds, but neither one of them wanted to be seen publicly together very much. "Bad luck if that happens," Warren said.

He would drink beer with Midge every few days at his hideaway in the abandoned building, but only one or two cans at a time. He said this was enough to get a "happy buzz on," but not enough to get drunk because they'd both be restricted to their wards if they were caught. They would gargle with mouthwash Warren bought downtown and he would smoke a cigarette after drinking. They kissed and hugged but didn't have intercourse because the meds Warren was taking prevented him from functioning very well. Neither one complained much, though – they were in love. Some ward staff did not believe him when he said he had a girlfriend, or that he was falling in love. One of the nurses eventually got word from her colleagues on the unit where Midge was housed that Midge had a boyfriend on another unit with whom she was in love. The nurses on Midge's unit surmised that this was contributing to pulling her out of her depression and a big factor in projecting that she would be discharged in June.

Coincidentally, Warren himself had just completed a testing battery at a vocational center, and in a team meeting in late May, there started to be more serious discussion of discharging him to a halfway house 20 miles away. Gina and the voc. rehab. counselor, who always came to the meeting at the end of the month, suggested that maybe Warren could work at a sheltered workshop near the halfway house, and an outreach worker from the mental health clinic could monitor his progress closely. Warren knew that Midge was supposed to be discharged to a group home not far from there, and when he was brought into the team meeting for a treatment plan review, he virtually begged for this to happen. He was given no guarantees by Dr. Dell, but this was the age of deinstitutionalization, and many patients who had been hospitalized for years were getting out to either family, or supervised settings not only to provide a better quality of life, but also because it would save the state quite a bit of money. After the team meeting, Warren went downtown to the Salvation Army and bought some clothes to prepare for moving out of the hospital and back into society. He felt confident that he would finally be discharged from the "bughouse" within a week or two, after all these years.

The next day, he met Midge at one of their semi-secluded places – on a bench in back of some trees near the softball field. She was there first and had a sad look on her face.

"I could be getting out at a place near you this month – isn't that great news! Hey, are you OK? You're starting to cry."

"I'm going home tonight."

"That's good! We might be at the sheltered workshop together pretty soon. What's so bad about that?"

"I'm not going to the group home. My mother wants me back. One of her friends is getting me a part-time job at a fabric store. I'm gonna be 40 miles away from you. I can't see you anymore."

Warren yelled, "What! When the hell did this happen? I had my whole life going well. I had everything planned for us. I can't go where you're gonna be. I don't know anybody there and that town is so small, I could never find a place to live!"

"I'm sorry, Warren, "she said with tears running down her cheeks. "I'll always care about you."

"So, you're getting rid of me, aren't you?"

"It's my family wanting this. I gotta do this if I want to get out of here, and they don't want me to have anything to do with anyone from the state hospital."

Warren got up and angrily staggered back to his building. He went right to his room, not acknowledging anybody. After doing some pacing and lying on his bed for the next half hour, he suddenly took a razor blade and slashed his left arm, pounding his door with his right fist and cursing loudly. One of the aides came to his room, yelled for nursing staff, and Warren was transferred STAT to the Medical/Surgical building. He had 18 stitches put in his arm. Luckily, there was no arterial cut, and he nicked only one vein. He stayed at the Medical/Surgical building for a couple of days and was transferred to the Maximum Security unit for 5 days until he was sent back to his geographical unit.

For the next 11 days, Warren refused to go to all activities, or to see Greg or Gina, or come to group therapy. He was belligerent toward staff, saying that he was "treated like a man at M&S, but treated like a throwaway at Maximum Security and here - like when I first came to the bughouse." His hygiene and appearance started to deteriorate again. Nursing staff said they suspected him of stealing articles from other patients (which was probably not true) and staff offices (he had occasionally, in the past, admitted to taking pens from the nurses' station). On June 21st he was ordered into the team meeting, after refusing to come a couple of times the week before. The plan was to talk to him first about the goals the team had for him. Greg spoke for the group.

"OK, Warren, basic things first – we want you to improve your hygiene, and clean and organize your room. Your hunger strike of the past several days is only defeating any hope you have of getting out of here – you were close to leaving a few weeks ago. You have got to start eating something every meal so you can get some nutrition into you – you're about 15 pounds underweight. You might weigh less than some of the jockeys at a race track. We want you to come to group therapy and see me for individual sessions twice a week – it doesn't have to be formal. It's your responsibility if you want any help I can try to give you. You're better off conforming to ward rules. We have rules that are less strict here than a lot of other units in the hospital. You were doing better last month when you were complying with all the ward rules. Don't start going on and on about grandiose stuff, like unrealistic things you can do or will do, or have done – much of the time staff will know you're lying and other patients won't like you for it. Most people won't take you seriously and they will even laugh AT you, not WITH you. That's also why some patients want to fight you. We want to see you get discharged at some point so that you can live in a group home and have some kind of steady work situation.

"Now about Midge – it sounds like she is gone out of your life. That's unfortunate. We understand that hurts, and what happened in that relationship is not on you. Together, you and I can work on these thoughts and feelings you have, and the behaviors related to them. You haven't interrupted and you seem like you're listening. Do you have any reaction to all this?"

Warren said, sullenly, "I'll start eating some, but I hate most of the state food. I'll come to your office and see you a couple of times a week. I can't promise anything else right now."

Patti, the nursing supervisor, asked, "Warren, you're still angry, aren't you?"

"I am. I just might stay at this bughouse until I die." He got up and left the meeting.

That afternoon, Warren dropped by Greg's office. He spent the first 10 minutes feeling sorry for himself because he wasn't like other people growing up. Then he started talking about how he had been the victim of persecution by the nursing staff for years. He stated, "I like doing what they say I can't do. The younger aides are mostly OK, but the older staff make me feel belittled, so I try to belittle them. I don't know if I want to get out of here or not anymore."

"It's a lot less stress and freedom if you're out of this place, but you're always gonna have some kind of authority to answer to, and rules to abide by, no matter where you live."

"I like fighting with them. I like it when I win."

"Do you ever really win in the long run? Maybe you win a little battle once in a while, but it sounds like you've been in a nine-year war here."

"In my mind, I don't give them the satisfaction of beating me."

"Put yourself in a different role. Say you were a staff member and you had to deal with somebody exactly like you day in and day out. How could you help Warren?"

"Treat him like a man and trust him. But I'd never want to work with patients in the bughouse. Maybe if I had a job at the Patio shop. That reminds me – until I get privileges to go off the ward, I have to ask Jim (an aide) to take me to the Patio Shop now before it closes. I have to get a carton of cigarettes, a jar of coffee, and deodorant. I want to eat two hot dogs and fries there instead of the crap they're gonna feed us tonight."

"We didn't discuss what happened with Midge yet."

"It's over. Period. I don't want to talk about it. I gotta go."

Several days later he came into Greg's office again. He immediately started getting grandiose about how he deserved to get unemployment benefits because he was no longer at the bookbindery. After Greg confronted him on how such contentions start arguments with others, he stated that he deserved to get a huge SSDI check for all the years he had been here, and he would talk to Gina about it. As Greg shook his head and rolled his eyes, Warren then quickly mentioned an inane scheme about how he could recruit 12 people to come to group therapy – even put up posters all over the building to advertise it, and of course, Greg would pay him for it. Then he started laughing, and Greg laughed with him.

Then he got serious. "I need money. I need better clothes. I got to be more acceptable to people."

"You just bought some clothes at the Salvation Army not long ago."

"They're too big. I lost weight. I was banking on putting on some pounds when I got out of here."

"Do you want a female viewpoint? Can I bring in Ms. Riendeau (Gina – whose office was across the hall)?"

"Yeah. I want to hear what girls think."

Greg went over and got Gina, who was not with any patients. A couple of minutes after she sat down, she rendered her opinion of how Warren could be optimally presentable to the "outside world."

"Warren, first you have to keep your hygiene up. Take a shower every day in the warmer months and at least every other day in the winter. Shampoo your hair and comb it. Keep the moustache if you want, but don't try to grow a beard – you have too many bare spots on your face."

"I want to keep the goatee."

"Then trim it."

Greg said, "It looks a little wretched." Laughter ensued by all.

She continued, "Make sure your pants fit. One pair of pants you wear looks a couple of inches too short. Another pair looks too baggy. Get rid of the old white socks – people only wear them with jeans and sneakers. When you're downtown, you want to blend in with others, not look like you're AWOL from the state hospital. Look around and see what other people are wearing the next time you're downtown."

"I'll try to do all that. People here steal clothes before they get discharged from this place, though. I'm tired of having to prove myself to people all the time."

"You can do it, though. You had a bad month, but you can start turning things around today – if you really want to," Greg said.

Chapter 6:
AN ORNERY SUMMER FOR WARREN

On July 1st, Warren argued with the nurses and aides all day. Terry, one of the aides, suggested he see Greg in his office, but Warren refused. Greg was at a continuing education conference in another building that afternoon, but when he returned, he found a note under his door that read:

> "I, Mr. Warren E. Le Blanc, by laws of this state, the bughouse that I am in, and the fact that I was adopted, will now only answer to the name Irish, and I hereby change my name to Mr. Ernest B. Irish. Inmate number 55303.
>
> These vows I make and intend to keep:
>
> I will never try to leave this hospital.
>
> I will remain a boozer and drug abuser.

If I can do it, I will not leave this ward I am put on now, unless forced.

I will no longer play any games (cards, pool, bingo, etc.) with any inmates.

I will try (hopefully successfully) to stay out of any cafeteria or eat state food unless it is a diet tray made up especially for me.

In general, I will do anything to stay here because I've been institutionalized for my unnatural life.

(signed) Ernest B. Irish.

Inmate #55303"

On Thursdays, Greg worked evenings. He had group therapy at 7 o'clock that evening with one of the aides serving as co-therapist. Six patients came, including Warren, surprisingly. Warren spoke only when spoken to, and he uttered only one- or two-word responses. Near the end of the session one patient stated that he was looking forward to being discharged soon so he could "get a job, get married, and settle down." As soon as he said this, Warren calmly got up and left the group. He refused to talk to Greg afterwards, but said he would write a note to Greg about his feelings. As Greg was leaving for the evening, the aide who was co-therapist in the group that night gave him the note. Warren wrote:

"I live on the banister of life, but it's all slivers. I've never lived free, but someday I will die free. Death is peace and rest. I'll never again want or give love, but love is death. Such beauty in death. The only things that are certain are birth and death. I have only one regret, but only one fear: death. I have these three wishes: Death. No more pain. Quick and painless.

No one to regret. All I fear is fear itself. I wish to die free. I also wish that no one mourn for me, remember me, or even care for me. I'm not worth living in anyone's thought, for I never want to do anything for anyone to ever remember me by.

I love and hate no one, including myself. This also goes for respect. Soon, hopefully, my wishes will become reality. A fond farewell, Irish."

Greg went to Warren's room. He wouldn't open the door, and said, "Just go away. Leave me alone."

Greg showed the note to nursing staff, and told them to call the O.D. (M.D. on call) and suggest that Warren be put on suicide watch, given his history of attempts. This was the first order of business in the team meeting the next day. Warren was put on a 24 hour 1 to 1 with ward staff for the next seven days. His medication was also changed. After five days, he started getting upset about still being on 1 to 1 status and restricted to the ward. He wrote another note to Greg, asking him to read it in tomorrow's team meeting. Warren wrote:

"I, Mr. Warren E. Le Blanc, known as Irish, declare the following:

I was restricted to the ward and put on 1 to 1. Because of this, I did not go to any individual or group sessions, and I am refusing to eat state food until the following are done: a. The restriction is lifted. b. Dr. Dell and staff apologize for what they have done. c. My right foot and leg get operated on, like they said they would. d. I no longer fall and hurt because of my foot and leg. e. I am given a high calorie diet that has no Ensure, no milk, no tomato juice, no oranges, no cooked tomato, no whole baked potato, no cheese, no codfish. f. Until these are done, I don't eat. No brag, just fact.

Irish."

On Friday, the new medication (Navane) started showing a significant positive effect for Warren, and his mood significantly improved. His hunger strike was over. Dr. Dell was leaving as Unit Director, and one of his last acts was to take Warren off restrictions after the weekend. Warren wanted see Greg in his office on Monday afternoon.

Greg asked him, "Were you seriously thinking about killing yourself the night you left group therapy?"

"No. I was feeling down in the dumps and I kept thinking about Midge after group that night, but I really wasn't gonna try to kill myself. It was more like I wished I was dead and might be better off that way. I really blew it out of proportion. I knew it'd be worse for me if I thought I'd fight getting off the 1 to 1, but at least I meant that last note was as a message for people to take me seriously, for a change."

"We have to take those notes you wrote seriously. Are you admitting that you blew things out of proportion just to get attention? You should know by now that's not the way to do it. Remember the assertive vs. passive-aggressive stuff we've talked about in group? Some of the stuff you wrote in the last note — the 'apology' and the hunger strike, most staff dismissed as grandiose. You and I have talked about how grandiose stuff doesn't help you in any interactions with people."

"Yeah. I'll admit it. I have problems with that. Sometimes it's all a front. A lot of times it's no brag, just fact, though."

"You said 'a front.' A front for.."

"Inferiorities."

"If you really believe that, I think that shows progress. You don't have to try to impress people with b.s."

He did not respond, but said he promised to see Greg in a therapy session next week, and that he would come to group twice next week.

In the next session, he said that things were going better for him lately. A new psychiatrist, Dr. Demetrius, took over as Unit Director and Warren got a chance to meet with him individually late one afternoon.

Warren said, "I like him so far. I like to make people angry when I'm starting any kind of relationship because you really know what a person is like when they express their emotions. That's what I did the first day I met you."

"So how did you try to get him upset?"

"I told him the medication I'm on is starting to give me side effects – dizzy, feel like I'm gonna fall. I demanded that he take me off it. He got my chart, looked at it and said he never liked for anyone to be on Navane, anyway, and he said he would take me off it.'

"You know, with most people, if you try to create a first impression that you're angry or demanding things from them, that will turn them off."

"Well, I judge people right then and there."

"I want you to think about how far that angry and demanding approach has worked for you toward getting out of here and improving your life."

About a week later Warren regained his grounds privileges, but the next evening after dinner he got into an altercation with a new patient and a fight was about to start. This resulted in him being restricted to the ward again. He wrote a note to Dr. Demetrius:

> "Just a few legal words to inform you about what hap-pened yesterday at about 6:30 p.m. I believe I had an epylitic (sic) fit which caused me to yell at a patient and go down to the floor. Then I slept for almost an hour and a half. I also felt like I was tasting lead coming out of my mouth. The same thing happened at 2:30 a.m. but I was uncontious (sic) for about a half an hour.
>
> No brag, just fact!
>
> Mr. Ernest B. Irish III"

This was discussed in team meeting the next day. Nursing staff on evenings and nights didn't believe Warren's note. He refused to show up for any individual or group sessions for the rest of the month until he would no longer be restricted to the ward.

Warren did write another letter to Dr. Demetrius at the end of July bizarrely requesting a large amount of many food items and condiments. He claimed that these were the only foods he could eat, but it was suspected by staff that he would try to somehow have another sandwich or lunch sale in back of the building to make money. Greg saw him briefly on the ward after Warren's request was brought up in team meeting. He denied that he was going to try to have another sale in back of the building, and with a big smile on his face, he limped away. Greg went on vacation for the next 3 weeks. Warren's combative behavior did not change for the next two weeks, and his restriction to the ward was continued.

Chapter 7:
TURNING THINGS AROUND?

Warren sulked through much of August. He refused to come out of his room to eat any meals except breakfast, sporadically walking out of various activity groups, and sometimes sneaking off the ward to go down to the Patio Shop. On one occasion in mid-August, at the Patio Shop, Warren made a deal with a patient from another unit who had off grounds privileges to buy a hand-held hole puncher for him. When the guy came back to the Patio Shop the next day, Warren got the puncher, went back to the building, and sold it for $15 to Bob, a friend of his downstairs on the Behavior Modification ward. Over the next few days, Bob (who knew where the punch cards were kept in the drawer at the nurses' station) and a couple of other patients on that ward started reaping the benefits of gaining a lot more points than usual on their punch cards. But Bob soon got caught with the cards and the puncher and confessed the whole scheme to staff. No more punch cards after that – they started a point system totally determined by nursing staff at the last team meeting of the week and kept in another drawer in the nurses' station. Warren was placed on 1 to 1 for four days until the team meeting the next Monday – he admitted the scheme, but he was angry that he couldn't get a patient payroll job or a part-time job downtown because he needed money. Even one of the nursing students from a regional program who was assigned to Warren for her 4-week psych. rotation confronted him on her last day and told him that his diagnosis really was a "passive-aggressive pain in the ass."

Right after that, Warren started cooperating more with staff for a few days and seemed to be in a better mood, according to the nurses in the team meeting on August 26th. Greg had just come back from vacation and remarked, "Maybe the untherapeutic 'street diagnosis' by that nursing student worked."

Cindy, the charge nurse, told Greg that Warren wanted to see him in his office at 3 o'clock, and Greg responded that he was free then.

As Greg opened his office door after coming back from lunch, a note from Warren was on the floor.

"Sir Edwin B. Irish III. Treatment Plan as of 3:00 p.m. August 26th, 1976:

Short-Term:

Forget the past.

Sign Voluntary re-commitment papers if necessary

Accept treatment here

Long Term:

Get a GED

Get a job

Start a new bank account at Indian Head Bank. Put all but $15 each week into the account, and ask for discharge when there is at least $1700 or more in the bank account.

Legally change name.

Signed,

Sir E. Bryant Irish III alias Warren Ernest Le Blanc."

Warren came in the door and sat down in Greg's office right on time. Greg said, "I got your note. This is what you want for a treatment plan. We can discuss it in the team meeting on Friday. Your formal treatment plan review is due on the 1st, anyway. You mentioned $1700 in a bank account – that means you won't get out of here until at least 1979. Staff tells me you seem happy the past couple of days."

"I meant to say $700."

Then he smiled and excitedly said, "I got a letter from Janet (a patient who had a 2 week pass pending discharge). She said in the letter that she missed me, thought I was a great person, admired me for fighting the ward staff, and even expressed some love for me, but she said she doesn't know what she wants out of any kind of relationship with me. I'm shocked. I didn't know she cared. I didn't know anybody cared."

"Well, did you write back to her?"

"Maybe I could marry her. She's even better looking than most of the nurses at this hospital."

"Aren't you getting way ahead of yourself here?"

"Yeah. I know. She's about six years older than me. It was her first time in this place. She's living with her father about 40 miles away. She feels better since she stopped taking her medication."

"It's possible she'll be back in the hospital, then. You've seen what happens to people who get out of here and then stop taking their meds. Most of them come back far worse than when they left. Almost every patient who's been in the group therapy sessions that you've been in with me admits that. I hope she turns it around and stays out. And I hope you do what you say you will on this plan you wrote."

"If she can get out of here, I can do it. It would be even better if we were both out of the bughouse and we could help each other out."

"So, what's the first thing you have to do toward getting out of here?"

"Like I said, accept treatment. But I also want to see Nancy to get back on a patient payroll job again. I want to talk to her the first thing in the morning."

"Good – do it. I know it's your life, but here's some direct advice: any improvement you make has to be sustained – stick with it. Don't let any minor setbacks destroy your progress. Think before you act. Don't blow things out of proportion. Write down some good and bad things that happen every day. It seems to release some of your anxiety or tension when you write things down."

On September 1st, as Greg opened the door to his office, there was a note from Warren:

> *"Decree of Irish:*
>
> *Last night at approximately 11:40 p.m. I saw the privilege list in the nurses' station. On the side of my name it said, "No Privileges." I have two choices: Stand in a corner for 24 hours in protest or get locked up for 48 hours. What perturbs me the most is that this time when I had my privileges taken away, it was by a "kangaroo court" of nursing staff because of an outright lie to make an example out of me in front of the new nursing students.*
>
> *But I'm making a third choice. Yesterday I met with Vocational Rehabilitation and they agreed to send me for further education and to start a patient payroll job to prove I can co-operate with other workers. So here are MY rules:*
>
> *Sleep, for I must be rested for work.*
>
> *Use the elevator because doctors say I would fall if I try to climb too many flights of stairs.*

Eat, possibly only at work and on Sundays.

Smoke – it relaxes my nerves.

Coffee – it relaxes my nerves.

Watch TV – it relaxes my nerves.

Play pool – it relaxes my nerves.

Nature calls, interviews, and appointments when necessary.

Have my social security card.

These are my laws for September, unless I am given full privileges. Otherwise, I will do almost nothing else.

No Brag, Just Fact!!!

Sir Edwin B. Irish III"

Warren came to the team meeting for his treatment plan review in his bathrobe. He spoke first and he was angry.

"They won't serve me in the cafeteria because I'm wearing a bathrobe. How many of you eat your breakfast with your bathrobe on? I want a meal by 3 o'clock today or I won't cooperate with any treatment plan or any program!"

Greg asked, "Warren, can I share what you wrote to me this morning?"

"Do it! Those are MY laws for the month." He got up and left the meeting.

After some brief discussion, it was determined that a few things precipitated his behavior and the outburst. First, earlier that morning he got into an argument playing pool with another patient and apparently another patient had tried to goad Warren into a fight with the player. It was alleged that Warren threatened to swing his pool cue at the patient he was arguing with. Ward staff sent Warren to his room, and the charge nurse immediately determined "No Privileges" for Warren. Just before this incident, Janet was re-admitted, and she was totally indifferent to Warren – she reportedly had been "high" in the manic phase after she stopped taking her meds and then suddenly came crashing down into depression by the time she was back on the ward. Then he was told just before he came into the team meeting that he could not get a job at the sheltered workshop unless he had his social security card. He didn't have one in his wallet.

After he left the team meeting, one nurse said she didn't believe that he ever had one. There was an argument between Nancy (the Occupational Therapist) and Pete (the Vocational Rehab Coordinator) about this. Dolph, Warren's new social worker (Gina had gone back to school in Virginia two weeks earlier), said that it should be at the Cashier's office, if he had one. Later in the day, the whole matter was resolved when Dr. Demetrius, the Unit Director, decided to give Warren his grounds privileges back, and wrote the order for Warren to start at the sheltered workshop ASAP.

Ten days later, Warren was doing so well working and cooperating with everyone that he was hoping to be discharged by the end of October. He told Greg, very logically and appropriately, "I go to work. I stay in my room or go out of the building when I can get away. I still have my hiding place in another empty building. I'm smoking, but I'm not drinking. I'll only play pool with people I know. I avoid certain nurses and aides if I can."

"Have you been interacting with Janet?"

"Not really. There's other fish in the sea."

For the rest of the month, Warren was appropriately dressed, showed appropriate (although sometimes grandiose) sense of humor frequently, and was doing very well at his job. He sneaked off grounds one Friday night to see a high school football game for the first time in 10 years. He re-kindled a relationship with Midge, who came back to her same unit in the Main building in the last week of September. Staff agreed that this was the best month he ever had, in terms of his behavior, mood, cooperation, and his job. He preferred to see Greg informally, and sessions were rather brief, but he came to group therapy at least once a week and participated well.

Another note from Warren was under Greg's door at the end of the month.

"I want full off grounds unrestricted privileges for the following reasons:

Cash my check.

Put some money in my bank account.

Go to the library.

Go Friday after work with Midge to eat a dinner or go to a movie downtown with her (Midge was about to be discharged to a group home downtown on Monday).

Escort Midge back to where she is living Mondays and Thursdays.

Do any shopping when necessary.

Be able to go job hunting, even at the state unemployment office. I need a job on weekends.

Be discharged to the group home where Midge is living sometime between Oct. 22, 1976 and Nov. 15, 1976.

No Brag, Just Fact!

Midge's Irish."

In the team meeting that day, it was decided to grant him full off grounds privileges, but he was denied permission, at this time, to try to work downtown on Saturdays.

That night, he got into a shouting match with some older night shift staff about staying up in his room after midnight. The result was that the nurse called the O.D. who agreed that he should be put into seclusion (locked time out room) with IM meds, which got Warren more combative and angrier. Dr. Demetrius called a team meeting and except for a couple of nurses, staff were upset at the way this was handled. A couple of people (Dolph and Jack – a new intern) brought up that Warren could potentially sue the hospital. Warren was ordered into the team meeting by

Dr. Demetrius and he was offered to be discharged ASAP, even today, if a placement could be found for him.

Shockingly, Warren replied, "Thanks Dr. D., but I can't go yet. I need to stay here until early or mid-November because of my financial situation."

Greg said, after Warren left the meeting, "He's either developed real good insight over the past 5 or 6 weeks or the prospect of really leaving has scared the hell out of him."

Chapter 8:

BIG PLANS SELF-SABOTAGED?

As Greg came into work on October 5th, he found a note under his door from Warren. The note read:

> "On October 25th, 1976, by my calculations, I will have $162.28. I will put $50.00 in the bank. Next time, 2 weeks later, I'll be able to put $110.00 in the bank. Third time, a week after that, I can put $50 more in the bank. A total of $210.00 in the bank six weeks from now. I can save up to $259.99 by November 23rd to buy an engagement ring for Midge. On December 24th, 1976, together we'll have $269.01 in the bank without interest; $282.46 with interest. Also, either on December 24th, 25th, or 26th we will be married. $159.99 for the wedding rings and $20.00 for the license. She wants to pay half. After she gets her engagement ring, we will start a joint account. In other words, for a $150.00

ceremony and license, with the ring, I'll spend $230.99. Alone I'll have $52.47 left. But she will have approximately $300.00 in the bank. In 6 weeks, she will have $200.00 more in the bank, making it $502.47.

Please tell them at the YMCA downtown that I would like to rent a room, per month, starting October 25th, 1976. For maybe 2 to 3 months, or 59 to 61 days. I'll pay by the month, then by the week. Please have them send me the rates as soon as possible. Thanks.

Sincerely,

"No Brag: Just Fact!?!"

Midge's Irish

P.S. See you Oct. 6th, 1976 at 4 p.m.

Greg brought the letter up in team meeting. Most of the staff laughed, except for a few who thought that in his own way, Warren seemed to really be making plans toward getting out of the hospital, although he and Midge would need lots of help. The consensus was that Warren and Midge would be better off in a group home, but everyone in the meeting seriously wondered if Warren could sustain appropriate behavior through Christmas.

He came into Greg's office a little after 4 p.m. the next day.

"Nobody said anything to me yet about my getting out of here with Midge and getting married. Did you hear anything?"

"You really need to talk to Dr. D. and Dolph. You can't make discharge plans like this all by yourself. It's good that you and Midge are together again, but getting married so quickly may be a recipe for disaster. Besides, in yesterday's meeting, almost all of us think that both of you would be better off in a group home together, as the best-case scenario, if that's even possible in this town."

He responded, in an irritated tone of voice, "Put us where you want, but when we're out of here we're FREE! It all boils down to money and how much we'll have to make it out there. I just got another part-time job Saturdays at a paint store downtown. I start this weekend."

"I have to tell the staff this. I hope Dr. D. approves. You better not lose your off grounds privileges."

"I need to get an ID as soon as possible. Here's all the information anyone needs to know about me."

He handed Greg a sheet of paper with his Social Security number, the name of the employer at his new part-time job, the ward phone number, his date of birth, height, weight, color of his hair and eyes, blood type, and where he was born. He also wanted this information sent to the YMCA downtown.

Greg said, "You should give this to Dolph, but I'll tell you right now there is no way he'll send this to the YMCA downtown – at least not in the near future. You can talk to Dr. D. and he'll listen, but I doubt if he'll approve of your getting a room at the YMCA as long as you're a patient here."

Warren then stormed out of the office, yelling something incoherently halfway down the hall.

Things went well for Warren otherwise, except that twice in October he had to go home early from his Saturday downtown job because he had seizures. He wouldn't say whether or not he was spitting out his Dilantin or whether the seizures were caused by fumes from mixing paint.

On October 25th, he came to see Greg, but this time he was grandiose right from the first words he said. He immediately stated that by this time next year, he and Midge would own a house, have a child, and probably buy a new car. Greg just shook his head and asked Warren about his job, rather than argue with him (as many people did whenever Warren uttered grandiose statements). Warren stated that he didn't get fired from his job, but it sounded to Greg like he was "hanging by a thread" with it. He and

Midge were still going strong together, though, and Warren was abiding by all the ward rules.

At the end of the session, he admitted that, "I can't move out of the hospital until I'm more financially secure. I need another part-time job, or a different one than what I have that pays more. I still have the patient payroll job, but they won't let me work more than 3 days a week."

"Hang in there and set your goals lower. It takes patience to get out of here sometimes, but the hospital seems to be committed to getting people out who don't really need to be here. It's good that you're working, but there are more factors than that which have to be in place to get out and stay out of here. You'd need a lot of support from community agencies. Talk to Dolph about that sometime."

"I just need a chance," he replied, as he got up and limped away.

Over the next couple of weeks, things took a turn for the worse for Warren. First, he had to quit his job downtown because he had another grand mal seizure. The next Saturday, after dinner, he had an angry argument with the evening shift staff for trading something he bought downtown to another patient in return for using that patient's pillow (He screamed at a nurse, "I've had the same damn pillow for years now!"). He bolted out of the building, found his way downtown to the railroad tracks, and decided to sleep in a boxcar. Police brought him back to the hospital at 4 a.m. Warren said, "Some hobo rolled me, took my wallet and glasses (which he wore while he was working) in the middle of the night." It was decided to restrict him to the ward instead of sending him to Maximum Security.

Warren refused to see Greg in his office, but Greg saw him briefly on the ward on Monday. He said to Warren, "That is NOT the way to get out of the hospital! You've been doing so well, don't blow it all!"

Warren gave Greg a dirty look, and limped away, not saying anything. His patient payroll job was cut to two days a week.

As Greg was leaving to go out of town for Thanksgiving weekend, Warren stopped him and said, "I'll go along with the program here, except for OT (Occupational Therapy)."

"What's wrong with OT?"

"I don't get along with Lee Anne Newman."

"That's ridiculous – everybody likes her. She's never complained about you, that I know of."

"She won't let me do things MY way."

"You know that song, 'You Can't Always Get What You Want?' Sounds like that applies to you. Think about it. I'm running out of excuses to defend you in the team meetings. Look at you now – you're dressed pretty shabbily again for the first time in a long time."

He ignored those comments, and asked, "Is it true Dr. D. is leaving?"

"Yeah, but I don't know exactly when his last day is."

"I need to talk to him after Thanksgiving. I'll see you in your office when I get back from work on Tuesday. At least I still have Midge. She's still in the bughouse."

"Tell you what - I'll call some people at her unit to see if Midge can come into the session with you, OK?"

"Yeah. I'd like that. That'll be good for you to see us together."

Chapter 9:
UNLIKELY DISCHARGE – WILL IT LAST?

The staff on Midge's unit didn't think it was a good idea for her to come to the therapy session with Warren. Warren said to Greg, "She didn't want to come to our building, anyway. Besides, I'm not feeling that great today, so let's make it short here."

"What seems to be the problem?"

"I didn't sleep much last night and I want to take a nap. I'll tell you this, though – I don't know if I want to get out of here until sometime this winter. I don't think I'll have quite enough money to make it by the end of the year. I want to try to get another part-time job downtown. But maybe I should get out soon because I know I can work full-time downtown with the right job. I want to do this on my own."

You've had kind of a checkered job performance at the workshop, the bookbindery, and the laundry. Are you sure you would be ready to try full-time work?"

"Most of the people who work at those places are crazy patients, and I'm not crazy. All I need are Midge, money, and a job, and I can make it out of the bughouse."

"It's good insight that you think you need to stay here a little longer so your finances are where you want them to be. It's more than that, though – you have to show you can consistently control your emotions and tell yourself "STOP!" when you have the urge to get grandiose or angry with others. But jumping into a full-time job if you get one would be like jumping into the river downtown this time of year. Or any time without a life preserver."

He got up to leave, smiled and said, "But I can swim!"

In team meeting Monday morning it was brought up that Warren was restricted to the ward all weekend. Apparently, late Friday afternoon, two nurses (one of whom had many run-ins with him) accused him of stealing a cue from the pool table in the dayroom. After discussing Warren's recent setbacks as well as some of the progress he made in the past year, the new unit Director, Dr. Presley, summoned Warren into the team meeting to learn his side of the story.

As soon as he walked into the room, Warren angrily yelled in the direction of Cindy and Patti, "First of all, I did NOT steal any cue from the pool table! My room was searched and torn up and they didn't find the cue – I'd never sell something like that, if that's what they were thinking. There are some nurses and aides here who don't ever want to see me leave this place, so they will lie to keep me here. These are the people who don't want me to look for a job downtown. I didn't have any problems with any people working in the paint store - it was the seizures from mixing the paint that forced me out. If I can get another job and have enough money, there's no reason for me to still be here after all these years."

Greg spoke for the group. "Warren, you have three options:

You can stay on this ward, but you have to earn off grounds privileges and we'll review your progress in a week. When you leave the ward for other places on grounds – like the Patio Shop or to see Midge – you have to tell us where you will be, and tell the truth. Stay out of the tunnels (the hospital had a tunnel system connecting various buildings – a lot of illicit activity among patients took place in this network from time to time. Warren, in the past, made some of his "deals" there). If you get caught off grounds, you'll be restricted to the ward.

You can go back to the Behavior Mod ward downstairs and earn privileges by building up points from the staff there.

Dolph will start working now on discharge planning for you to get into a group home, and it might not be downtown – it could be anywhere in the southern part of the state. You'll have start-up money and an appointment at a county mental health clinic at their day treatment program, and you'll have a case manager to check on your progress."

"None of this is fair," he loudly responded. He pointed to Greg and said, "I'll see you this afternoon after lunch." He got up and left the meeting.

At 1 o'clock, he stormed into Greg's office, stating, "You people can't restrict my privileges for something I didn't do. You can't just throw me out of the hospital to someplace I don't want to go to, either. I'm never going back to the B-Mod ward. That'd be like a life sentence."

Greg asked, "Do you seriously want to get out of here, Warren? I wonder if you're scared to be discharged from here after being here for such a long time. It's OK to admit that, if that's what it really is."

"I was supposed to renew my name on the list at the YMCA today."

"Do not leave this office. I'm dialing the YMCA right now."

Greg called the YMCA Residence Director. The man told Greg that, "No one by that name (Warren Le Blanc) has put his name on our waiting list in November or December."

Greg thanked him and hung up.

Warren then screamed, "I'm gonna call a lawyer! You're nothing but a bullshit artist!"

Greg countered, "Look, Dolph can help discharge you the proper way so you can get the right amount of help and support. I suggest you see him."

"I'm calling the Human Rights Commission, too!" He limped out of Greg's office as fast as he could.

A few hours later, Willard Paul, the hospital attorney and Fran Gervin of the state Human Rights commission, called Greg. Greg explained the situation and generally what had happened with Warren in the past few weeks. They dismissed Warren's complaint.

Over the next week and a half, Warren cooperated well with the staff. He met with Dolph and agreed to possibly be discharged soon to a shared apartment with Midge downtown ("If I can swing it, Warren," Dolph said.). The setting would be about 4 blocks away from the hospital and right near the mental health clinic. Dolph somehow could get him startup money from Welfare (SSDI? Social Security Disability Insurance?) ASAP.

On the morning of December 16th, Dr. Presley met with Greg and Joan White, Warren's main adversary of all the nurses on the ward. Dr. Presley felt that from listening to Joan White that instead of being discharged, Warren should be considered for transfer to the Maximum Security unit. Joan White told Dr. Presley this because, "His emotions are out of control and he is a potential danger to himself."

Dr. Presley turned to Greg and said, "He fails to get along with most of the patients and staff, and he said to someone in the nurses' station today, 'What do you want me to do – jump off the roof?'"

As Joan White slyly smiled, Greg turned to her and said, "I was down the hall and I overheard that argument he had with you and another patient. Warren said that comment in a matter-of-fact way, with no emotion or conviction in his voice."

Dr. Presley said to Greg, "I want you to talk to him about staying here for a while. He has a sinus infection that spread to his right ear and he just got dental work done. He's complaining of a headache now."

Greg replied, "My gut feeling is that this place is giving him a headache and might be sabotaging any progress he's made. I hope you give him a chance to be discharged. I suspect he's not suicidal. He may have some high anxiety about getting out of here after all these years. He needs a chance, in my opinion. I'll see him right now."

It was a 45-minute emotional, tearful session for Warren with Greg. He anguished over the fact that not only are the majority of the staff mistreating him, but one newer patient in particular, Chuck, has been riding him hard – saying everything he says and does is "full of crap," and telling Warren that he "isn't worth a shit as a person."

Warren sobbed, "He keeps telling me in front of all the patients that, 'It's a tough world out there, boy. You're never gonna make it.' Why can't people treat me like a man instead of a kid? It's bad enough for staff to put me down, but on the ward now, almost all the patients are against me, too."

Greg asked, "Do you ever think, 'What kind of things do I say or do that turn other people off toward me?' What about your social skills?"

He cut Greg off and said, 'No, I don't really believe there's a problem with that at all. I still say, 'No brag – just fact.' But I mean it. I made a lot of enemies here, but I have some friends. I got respect from some people who have come and gone from the bughouse for fighting the staff. Some people are even jealous of me because they're afraid to say what they feel to staff."

"Saying what you feel is good, but there are right ways and wrong ways to do it. Remember all the times in group therapy we talked about being assertive instead of aggressive or non-assertive? Or what it means to be passive-aggressive? What about how much you value the opinions of other people? You have to decide if there's a grain of truth regarding others' opinions of you, or whether it's all crap. How much can you really do for yourself, and are there times when you really need help? Do you think about all those things?"

"Maybe I'm over the top and get too emotional once in a while," he said softly.

Greg said, "It's tough growing up in a state hospital, but you have a chance to move on."

"I think I got fired from my job (at the sheltered workshop) today," he said with resignation in his voice.

Greg called the workshop. Warren's supervisor said that he was suspended temporarily, pending an "OK" from Dr. Presley, because he was angrily complaining about the equipment. After Greg hung up and related this information, Warren seemed much calmer. They went back to see Dr. Presley.

Dr. Presley said to Greg, "I'd like you to go to a hearing to get him (Warren) involuntarily committed."

Warren and Greg were shocked. Greg yelled out, "Why?"

To Warren he said, "The more I think of it from what Joan said, you might be a danger to himself. You made a suicide attempt once by jumping off the roof of the building next door."

Warren yelled, "That was, what do you call it, taken out of context! I'm not gonna do that!"

Warren got up to leave, and Greg also stood up. As Greg went out the door, he said to Dr. Presley, "Please reconsider your decision. We're going to talk to Dolph right now."

Dr Presley replied, "I'll make a final decision tomorrow in team meeting, but Warren, you're still restricted to the ward."

"Don't say anything," Greg said to Warren in a low voice.

When they got to Dolph's office, there were two other social workers in his office – Mary Lynn and Jeffrey. Greg told them what happened in the meeting with Dr. Presley. Mary Lynn, who worked with Dr. Presley for several years on another unit, said that most of the time before he makes an important decision, he seriously listens to the last person who talks to him. Jeffrey, who worked on another unit in a different part of the building, said that he knew the YMCA downtown had several vacancies in their residential component and he was able to get a patient discharged to there later today with the blessing of his unit director. Dolph told Warren that he couldn't get both him and Midge into the shared apartment downtown (there were three other former hospital patients there), but he was able to get one of the rooms at the YMCA for him to move in on Monday, if Dr. Presley agreed and (to Warren) if you cooperate with everyone here and keep your nose clean until then.

"I'll talk to Dr. Presley before I leave today," Dolph said.

"Can I give a notice to sign out of here AMA (Against Medical Advice)? Some other people got out of here that way," Warren asked.

Dolph replied, "Technically you can do that, but if you don't have a placement and other things like a clinic appointment and finances set up, Dr. Presley will try to get you committed involuntarily here. Let me handle this. If all goes well, I'll see if they can take you at the YMCA tomorrow or Monday morning for sure."

Warren sneaked off the unit after this and met with Midge. They went to Warren's hideaway in the abandoned building and they talked for about an hour, as she told him her plans for discharge the next day. That night, Warren wrote a letter to be presented at team meeting in the morning. It read:

> *"To all staff here:*
>
> *I sincerely apologize for my behavior and moodiness for the time you knew me. Please realize my heart is with Midge, and I desire to be with Midge as soon as possible. Then all the time. Dr. Presley and Mrs. White, I definitely have to apologize*

to you, both for my moodiness and carrying on. I will not let the Legal Aid attorney take on my case. Tomorrow after the Community Meeting I desire to go to the Treatment Room for a very needed check on my right ear.

I include that I have no suicidal tendencies and I still desire my discharge tomorrow, December 17th, 1976. I believe I can do a lot better on the outside. Also, at 9:45 on Monday, I have an interview to be restarted at the sheltered workshop. Thank you, Greg and Dolph for helping me. Again, I apologize to any people I hurt. To Dr. Presley and Mrs. White, I hurt and threatened you the most. I rushed to too many conclusions. I should have realized the trouble and time it would take for putting me on suicidal precautions. Please forgive these truly unforgivable errors.

Highly idiotic but apologizing,

Sir Warren E. LeBlanc Esq."

Warren's letter was read at the end of team meeting the next day. There was arguing regarding whether he should stay in the hospital or be discharged, but Dr. Presley said that he wanted to meet with Greg, Dolph and Warren in his office after Warren got back from the Treatment Room. They met at 11 o'clock. Warren said he had a mild ear infection but it would be fine in a couple of days, and he was ready to be discharged. Dolph said that he got Warren a room at the YMCA downtown to move in that day, and an appointment at the mental health clinic on Tuesday afternoon. Dolph also heard that Midge was moving into her shared apartment today, which was a couple blocks away from the YMCA.

Dr. Presley agreed to discharge Warren AMA, and he gave him a two-week prescription for Dilantin, the only medication Warren was taking at the time. Dolph and Greg took him to his room downtown at the YMCA. They wished him a Merry Christmas, as Warren smiled and waved.

Greg wrote his discharge summary as soon as he got back to his office. For "Prognosis," he put, "Guarded to poor." But he hoped that he would be wrong.

Chapter 10:
THE "REVOLVING DOOR" STARTS

Warren spent much of the time over the Christmas holidays with Midge. The only time he went back to the hospital was to retrieve what leftover things he had from out of his hideout in the abandoned building, which he accomplished without getting caught. Midge had begged him not to go back and do this. She seemed slightly more distant to him in the time leading up to the end of the year, starting with the day after Christmas, when her family members took her home to visit for a few days.

Things came to a head on New Year's Eve. Warren and Midge were near the end of dinner at a Chang's, a Chinese restaurant downtown. Midge suddenly got tearful.

"I can never marry you," she quietly said.

"What? Why!"

"A lot of reasons. I thought about it all week."

Warren angrily said, "Your family's against me!"

"Yeah, but we can't afford to have kids, we can't afford a car, we can't even afford to get a good apartment to live in, and we don't even have full -time jobs. It'll take years for us to make it out here. I'm sorry, Warren. I don't want to do it, but we have to break up. I can't see you anymore," Midge said, crying.

Warren was angry. He got up, slammed down his dish and threw money at her, yelling, "Here – Happy New Year!"

Warren limped out of the restaurant and went back to his room at the YMCA. He swallowed all the medication he had, even the over the-counter aspirins and vitamins, and chugged a pint of Old Crow he had bought to share with Midge later. Warren woke up in the local hospital and the next day he was transferred back to the state hospital at the Neurology Unit.

Greg came back to work on January 3rd, after being out of town for the Christmas and New Year holidays. Just as he was about to go into the team meeting, Terry, one of the aides, told him that Warren was in the general hospital in town, according to her boyfriend, who was a nurse in the ER there. She didn't know any of the details, however. In the team meeting, a call came through to Dr. Presley from the Director of the YMCA who related to the unit staff that the YMCA didn't want Warren back because they felt he could not live independently. He told the staff that Warren made a suicide attempt and currently he was in the Neurology Unit. Greg was in Dr. Presley's office later in the day discussing a matter concerning another patient, when Dr. Presley told Greg that Warren would be in the Neurology Unit for days, if not weeks, according to Dr. Mac Duff, the Neurology Unit Director.

"I really thought he had a chance to make it, if he could just stay out of here through the winter," Greg said.

Dr. Presley shook his head and responded, "We're getting too many patients out of here too soon. If he gets out again, he has to go to a supervised setting."

A week later, Warren wanted to get out of the Neurology Unit. He argued every day with Dr. Mac Duff about "robbing me of my freedom," and "some nurses and aides here are breathing down my neck with no respect for privacy." He made the impulsive decision to try to hang himself with a bed sheet – the knot broke almost immediately, and staff found him about 10 seconds after he tried this. He screamed that he wanted Dr. Mac Duff to send him back to his regular unit. Instead, they sent him to Maximum Security. Five days later, he got into a fist fight with another patient, which dashed any hopes of coming back to his regular unit soon. At the end of January, Warren was caught trying to escape at the change of day and evening shifts. He was caught by Security police just as he made it to the back of the Main Building.

In mid- February he wrote Greg a letter:

> *"Greg: Please forgive me for what I've done previously. Let me start anew. In laymen's terms, help!!!*
>
> *I desire to speak with you now. I'm OK, but so tired of being an 'escape goat.'*
>
> *My goals now are quite simple. I desire to get a part-time job. I want to go for discharge. Hopefully get Midge back. Appreciate and desire a reply, as soon as possible.*
>
> *Sincerely and truthfully,*
>
> *Sir Warren Le Blanc, Esq."*

Greg received the letter in the hospital mail the next day. He called Dr. Rex, his colleague at the Maximum Security Unit, who said that Warren would probably be there for about another two weeks. He related that Warren had shown improvement, but it might not be a good idea to come over and see him yet. Greg asked for Dr. Rex to tell Warren that he would see him in his office as soon as he got back to the unit. Warren returned from Maximum security in early March, but Greg had taken four days of leave and was out of town. A letter from Warren was under his door when he arrived back at work on March 7th. It read:

> *"Greg!!!*
>
> *I'm being held here against my will. On what grounds? I'm not a threat to society nor any longer a threat to myself. So therefore, I ask for an unconditional discharge.*
>
> *I, myself, was once told by a lawyer that 'bones stop growing at 25 years of age,' and therefore, on that ground alone, I may press charges on the Hospital because of my foot and my leg. It happened.*
>
> *Sincerely,*
>
> *Sir Warren E. Le Blanc, ESQ"*

Greg had a long session with him that afternoon. He did not seem suicidal or grandiose, although he was loud and argumentative at times.

Warren yelled, "I can't understand why Dr. Presley wanted to commit me involuntarily!"

"Easy, Warren. I want you to tell me as calmly as possible exactly what happened after Dolph and I left you at the YMCA just before Christmas."

"No, I'm not gonna give you all the details on what happened – that's between me and Midge. I'll just say that on New Year's Eve we were having dinner at Chang's when all of a sudden, she wanted to break up with me and never see me again. She gave me a lot of reasons why. I got mad, smashed my plate down on the table, threw money at her to pay for dinner and went back to my room and chugged a pint of bourbon. I woke up in the hospital. I remember going to the Neurology Unit here and I didn't like Dr. Mac Duff, so I made that suicide attempt so I could get sent back here. I didn't really want to kill myself, but it backfired on me, and they sent me to Maximum Security. A few days later they transferred David from our unit there, and I got into a fight with him because I thought he was trying to steal my coat. A week later I tried to escape, but I didn't make it out of the building. I'm finally OK now, and I want to get discharged from here again."

"This letter you wrote to me two weeks ago (Greg presented the letter to him) – those are your goals, right?"

"Yeah."

"So, what's the first step you have to do toward achieving these goals, if you can?"

"I've gotta sign out of here and live alone in the community. I have friends who are ex-patients who are living downtown or in other places. I'm not suicidal."

"You're getting way ahead of yourself. You're still Involuntary here. So what do you have to do first? Think!"

"I have to take my meds when they give them out. I have to go to all my activities. I have to get my privileges back. And I have to control my temper, but it's easier at this place if I have privileges so I can get away from most of these jerks as much as I can.

"After all these years here, you should know that you can't always get what you want when you want it. It's one step at a time."

Warren said, "And another thing – I called the YMCA today from the nurses' station. Most of my things are still there. I want them back. I don't have any money. The State Department of Welfare told me I could get SSI (benefits), but I wasn't out of the hospital long enough to get SSI. While I was living at the YMCA, I tried to look for jobs but nobody would hire me because of my physical condition."

"I'll talk to Dolph about getting your stuff back from the Y. I can bring up about you getting back your old patient payroll job at the book-bindery in team meeting, but it'll be a hard sell. You're gonna need a better support system than what you had."

"Thank you. I'd like that. You're right about support out there. I didn't like the lady (counselor) at the clinic they assigned me to. I wouldn't've gone back for another session with her. She seemed to talk down to me. Really, the only support I had was Midge. I'd like to talk to her. She's still living downtown, I hear."

"Step by step, Warren. Convince the staff here that you're improving by cooperating with the program and controlling your anger – assertively, not aggressively – especially when you talk to Dr. Presley. Then maybe he'll let you sign a Voluntary. Then soon you might get your privileges back. Then soon after that, maybe you can get your patient payroll job again and do well. If that goes well, we could plan for getting you out of here again. It won't be next week or even next month, probably. I have to go to a meeting now. I'll see you again Wednesday afternoon."

The next morning Warren got into a loud argument with Joan White about whether or not he was "cheeking" the meds that she gave him. His anger swelled past his "boiling point" and he picked up a chair and slammed it against the Nurses' station window. He was promptly sent off to the Maximun Security unit again. This time he remained there for 3 weeks.

Greg got a letter from him on March 23rd. It read:

> "Greg:
>
> Please get my possessions from the YMCA, if they're still there because I never got them all. Also find out who has my ruby-opal ring, military watch and my wallet. Real important to me, is to be able to go to school Monday and Thursday evenings to fulfill my GED. Important to me is to call Midge. Please!!!
>
> Sincerely,
>
> Sir Warren E. Le Blanc, Esq."

He came back from Maximum Security the next day. During his first week back, he was like a model patient. At the end of March, Dr. Presley agreed to give him grounds privileges. Matt, the hospital's Public Relations Director, called Greg early that afternoon, and told him he met Warren outside of the Library on grounds. Warren related to Matt that Midge "was pregnant after she was raped a few months ago." Matt suggested that Warren talk to Greg about this matter. Surprisingly, Warren came right over to Greg's office. Warren told him he found a phone number where Midge could be reached, and they talked for "a while" last night.

"She's still living downtown and doing babysitting for an ex-patient friend of hers. Making a living that way and getting SSI, too."

"What about this 'getting raped and getting pregnant'?"

"I think she was playing games with me. I want her to come over here this weekend and see me. She said she'll meet me on grounds and we both agreed we still care about each other. The pregnant thing was the last straw that got me upset on New Year's Eve. I never told you that because I was too embarrassed. If she did get pregnant, it wasn't by me. At least I don't think so. I wonder if she had another patient before she left and then she told me she got raped. Anyway, I don't believe it. I'll find out when I see her if she's pregnant."

"Does any of that change things about her for you?"

"No. I'm still in love with her. I want to get out of here and have another chance."

Greg gave him a lot of support and encouragement for how well he was doing. They agreed he was off to a good start this time toward accomplishing his goals of off grounds privileges, a patient payroll job, getting a GED, and getting discharged by the end of the spring. No expressions of grandiosities in the session.

The next week he came to group therapy twice for the first time in months and participated very well. The main topics of both sessions concerned anticipation of consequences of behavior and dealing with anger. On Friday, he was brought into team meeting for his treatment plan review, and he seemed relaxed, and related to everyone appropriately, even smiling a couple of times. After he left, Dr. Presley and Dolph remarked that this was the "best he's been since late last year."

In team meeting the following Monday morning, it was business as usual. The first hour involved discussion of three new patients who had come into the unit over the weekend. The next hour was devoted to another patient's treatment plan review. Cindy (who was now the supervising nurse) called out names while flipping through the Kardex as we briefly discussed the remaining patients on the ward. The meeting was about to adjourn when Greg asked, "What about Warren? You didn't mention him at all."

"Cindy replied, "Didn't you hear? He's back in Maximum Security for what he did Friday night with the knife."

Greg, Dolph, and Jack (the psychology intern) all seemed taken aback, as Greg asked, "What knife?"

Dr. Presley said, "I got a call from ward staff Friday night that Warren got a steak knife and told another patient that he would stab the first person who came into his room that night. The OD (M.D. on call) was contacted. Warren got into a heated argument with Joan White, Bill (an aide), and David (one of the patients), and they sent him to Maximum Security."

Later in the day, Greg talked briefly with David who said, "I didn't know whether he was kidding or serious – you can never tell with him. I told Johnny (another aide) and Bill. Johnny talked to Joan White, who brought Bill with her to talk to Warren. You know Bill is a big guy and she probably had him in there for protection. Warren and Joan can't stand each other. A half an hour later he was gone out of here screaming, with Security guys holding him."

As Greg was leaving work, he saw Johnny and asked what happened with Warren. Johnny said that David thought that Warren really had a knife, and when Joan confronted him, he refused to talk to her. She called the OD, and thought Warren might be a danger to others, and that's when

Warren was sent to Maximum Security. The knife was never found. Greg wondered what the real story was, as he walked out the door.

As Greg came back from lunch on April 21st, he noticed a note under his door, which read:

> "Greg!
>
> Is it so wrong to have human emotions, thus a desire to get back on off grounds privileges, when a lie has been fabricated to get me locked up for 11 days?
>
> I personally told Cindy that I had no knife. Also, Security guys, the aides, and Dr. Presley. They found no knife.
>
> I could have possibly finished my GED, gone for my job interview last Thursday at 3 to 4 p.m. at State Unemployment, got a duplicate of my Social Security card at the Federal Building, etc., etc., etc., etc.
>
> Is it so wrong!?!
>
> Sir Warren E. Le Blanc Esq.
>
> P.S. Only hearsay from patients?!?
>
> 4-21-77"

Warren came into Greg's office later that afternoon and ranted about being "railroaded" by ward staff allegations. Greg told him that he talked to David and Johnny, but Joan was off duty. Warren said, "Joan has had it in for me for years."

Greg didn't argue with him. Most of the staff thought Joan was marginally competent and could seem downright evil at times, but Joan had the support of two female aides who usually worked with her, and Cindy (Patti had left for another unit several months earlier). Greg knew Bill was out on the ward, so he called him into his office.

Bill said, "I only have a minute to talk because I just got pulled to another unit for the shift. Warren, we know your history, how angry you can get, and we didn't want to take any chances with you and a knife."

Warren angrily replied, "That's all hearsay!"

"You wouldn't give up the knife," Bill countered.

Warren yelled, "I never had a knife! That's hearsay!"

Bill said, "I've got to go," and left.

Greg said to Warren, "If you really didn't have a knife and you lied to David about having one, then this would be an example of how grandiosity and lying gets you into trouble."

Warren angrily replied, getting up from the chair, "I'm gonna call a lawyer and bring everyone in this building into court!"

He slammed the door and left. Greg wondered if he made an untherapeutic remark and could have handled it better.

Warren showed up for his therapy session the next day but stayed for only half of the allotted time. Greg asked, "Do you feel that the situation with the so-called knife has been resolved and you can move on with your life now?"

"There never was any goddamn knife! If those bitches out there in the nurses' station want to play games with me, I'll play games with them! And I'll beat them!"

"Has that approach ever helped you toward getting out of this place?"

"I'll get out of here someday in a pine box. On my terms."

"Tell me seriously – are you thinking of any plans to try to make a suicide attempt?"

"No. Not now. But it's frustrating dealing with these people – most of the staff and certain patients here. I'm not being treated like a human being! I don't even know where Midge is now. She's not living at the same place downtown."

Warren then went into a long rant – first, a litany of all the physical problems he had that he claimed were never treated properly at the state hospital. He then declared that the ward staff and the Cashier's office had confiscated almost all of his possessions and that they blocked all of his plans for improving his life and getting out of "the bughouse." Greg handed him the phone in his office and gave him the number of the hospital Cashier's office to call, but Warren refused.

"You have nothing to lose by calling them," Greg said.

"I've had enough of this," he replied. "I'll see you in the morning and call them then."

"Dolph is your social worker. He could help you with this better than I can."

The next morning Dolph was in court, so Greg again offered Warren the opportunity to call to the Cashier's office. Someone responded and acknowledged that they did have some of his things but could not return them to him until he was discharged. He became loud and belligerent and said to whomever was on the phone, "You don't know what the hell you're doing!" He slammed down the receiver.

He got up to leave, saying, "I have to go and see Lisa (Unit Business Manager). I'll see you next Tuesday. I'm not coming to group anymore."

Warren didn't show up for another session with Greg until May 10th. Several days before that, it was noted in team meeting that he seemed calmer and more cooperative. In the session he seemed to be in good spirits, but suddenly got grandiose when talking about a "wealthy" grandfather who had all the same ailments as him and lived to be 106. Warren said his goal in life now was to outlive him. Then, while he was discussing his need to see a dentist, he angrily brought up how he was mistreated over the knife incident.

"Warren, isn't that over and done with?"

"Yeah, but the point is, you're not supporting me enough in my battles with the staff out there. I hope in team meeting tomorrow you will recommend me for off grounds privileges."

Team meeting members were split for and against this, but Dr. Presley, making the final decision, said that they should wait one more week. When Warren heard of this, he refused to see Greg until two weeks later. At that time, he came by Greg's office stating that he agreed to participate in a project with a few other patients who were to move out as a group into a shared apartment in another part of the state in a few months. Greg knew that Dolph was the administrative head of this project, with graduate student Jack Orvis and Gina (who had just returned to the hospital for the summer after being away at graduate school) as the main facilitators for this project.

Warren said, "I was talking to staff here about this kind of an idea two years ago. I heard Dolph's wife was involved in getting a couple of patients out of here in a situation like this. I'll see Jack for sessions, but I'll stay in touch with you."

"OK, lets you and I make it informal. You're always welcome to come to group therapy, though.

Chapter 11:
THE REVOLVING DOOR CONTINUES

Warren was granted his off grounds privileges again by the third week of May. He went downtown to look for Midge and encountered a few other former patients over the next few days, but they didn't know where she was living. The residence where Midge was staying refused to tell Warren where she now was located, and a letter he sent to her came back "Return to Sender. Not At This Address." He sadly figured that Midge was gone out of his life forever.

However, he was doing very well on the unit and in training for the shared apartment program. There were a few incidents where he got into angry verbal outbursts with Jack and Gina for bending or breaking the rules of the program, mostly connected with going off grounds and missing meetings. Greg suggested that Jack let the group decide any consequences. On Jack's last day of his internship, before he was hired as a mental health worker at the clinic in the town to where the group was relocating (part of the deal was that Jack would still be the main administrator for the program; Gina was still at the hospital), the group had a meeting to decide if Warren should continue with them. They unanimously voted "Yes." Warren's only communications with Greg were brief and informal after Jack left, and he did not want to discuss any anxiety he was feeling over his impending discharge with the group.

Due to some administrative conflicts, Warren and three other patients were discharged to an apartment 55 miles away from the hospital, but a block away from where Jack was now living, near the mental health clinic. Unfortunately, the shared apartment program fell apart after five days. The main reason for this was that one of the former patients in the group was not only manic-depressive and refused to take his medication, but he was also an alcoholic and a sociopath. He started drinking in the apartment right away. This man challenged Jack's authority from the first day, and ended up getting in a fist fight with Jack and going to jail. Two ex-patients in the group had psychotic breaks as a result of the chaos and went back to the hospital. Warren, who was spending much of his time exploring the community and trying to see if he could find some other ex-patients who lived in the town, "weathered the storm" and Jack and Gina arranged to have him move into a boarding home not far away from the apartment. Warren participated in the clinic's resocialization program, had sessions with Jack at the clinic twice a week, went to the YMCA a couple of days a week, and attended church on Sundays. He thanked Jack for sparing him any excuse for returning to the hospital and was grateful for "the chance to live a normal life again." Gina went back to school in Virginia to finish her MSW degree.

Warren continued to do fairly well for the first two weeks of September, being helpful to others at the boarding house and in the clinic's groups that he attended. Jack's sessions focused mainly on Warren's late transition into becoming an adult and overcoming the effects of the years of institutionalization. However, Warren started to have some brief loud outbursts concerning rules of the boarding house when he was stayed out late and refused to tell anyone where he had been. In mid-September, he made a suicide attempt by ingesting an unknown quantity of medications. There were two precipitating stress factors for this. First, a lady stood up Warren for his first date since New Year's Eve with Midge. Then, as he angrily walked back into the boarding home from downtown, his landlady pulled him aside before he went to his room.

"Warren, today I talked to one of the doctors at the clinic about the possibility of you living somewhere else. You don't really fit in with the other residents here."

"What? You want to get rid of me?"

"The other people here are a lot older; you're coming in late a lot, you don't get up out of bed early, and it's better for you if you were somewhere else."

He yelled, "Leave me alone. I'm not going back to the state hospital or anywhere else. I earned my right to be free." He slammed the door to his room, swallowed the medication, and started sobbing. Soon his landlady went back to talk with him, and she heard a thud. When she opened the door to his room, he was lying on the floor. She called an ambulance, and he was admitted to the local hospital.

His stomach was pumped, and he was put on suicide watch. The next morning, a doctor making rounds interviewed him.

"How are you feeling today, Mr. Le Blanc?'

"Shitty, but I want to get out of here."

"You're not going anywhere today, but you can't go back to where you were living."

"I'm not going back to the damn state hospital. I'll burn down this whole ward if you try to send me back there!"

"Look, with the meds you took, you made a serious suicide attempt."

"No, I didn't really want to kill myself. I just had a miserable day and to top it off, I got stood up on a date. I'll behave. I'll do anything you say to get better. Where's Jack Orvis? He's my therapist at the clinic. Is he coming to see me?"

"He knows what happened. He'll be here this afternoon. You're not in any condition to go anywhere. You'll be on Observation status for a while, but we won't send you to the ICU. You're right next to the nurses' station. Cooperate with everybody. Don't mess with the IV. If you need anything, we're here to help."

Jack came by later in the afternoon. "Warren, what the hell happened?"

Warren told him the story and said, "Right now I feel like crap. At least everybody here has been nice, so far."

"We have to find another place for you to live. Hospital staff says you're gonna be here for about a week. That overdose of all those meds you took could have been deadly. You could have called the crisis line first."

"No, I was too upset and I just wanted to blot out everything."

"That's exactly WHY you should call the crisis line in situations like that. I know it'd be awkward to call from the boarding home, but you have a pay phone a couple of houses away on the corner. I'm sure Greg told you many times when you're upset like this, think before you act."

"Yeah. I heard it before. She's throwing me out and I need somewhere else to live. They're not gonna send me back to the bughouse, are they? Please don't let them do that. Can you get my stuff for me?"

"I'll do that. I'll try to convince whoever I can not to get you committed involuntarily. I'll talk to Vance (social worker at the clinic – the liaison person Warren's unit to the state hospital) to see if we can get you another placement quick."

"Thanks, Jack."

Warren was discharged a week later, and true to his word, he behaved very well. Vance got him into a group home not far away. However, over the next three weeks, he inconsistently attended his scheduled activities, despite Jack's attempt at close supervision. Warren called Jack in the evening once a week instead of the crisis line and talked about feeling like stabbing himself. He overdrew his checking account and wrote two bad checks – Jack bailed him out.

In mid-October Warren showed up at the clinic 20 minutes late to see Jack in a somewhat disheveled state. Jack had a long session with him. Warren told him he felt "defeated," and, "I'm having a tough time making it out here." At the end of the session, Warren grudgingly agreed to be admitted back to the state hospital, but "on a Voluntary. I don't want to be committed. You have to assure me that the stay there will be temporary, and not long-term."

"OK, that might be best for everyone."

He was brought into team meeting the day after he got back to the state hospital, and he seemed depressed. "I feel like a failure, but I don't want to be a failure. You know from what they wrote about me and from what Jack Orvis told Vance (who was present in the meeting) that I didn't want to die when I took those pills last month. I don't want to talk about that. I just had a bad period out there. I want to get out of here pretty soon – not months from now."

Greg saw him for a session that afternoon. Warren said, "I just need a rest. Get my head together, you might say."

"We are hoping that if things go well, you can get back to where you were in a couple of weeks. But it's mostly up to you. Like I said in the past, it's probably about 30% me and 70% you in a therapist-patient relationship."

"I know how to play this game better at the bughouse now. I got out of here twice since last Christmas. Yeah, you can help me. I think you have in the past. Jack tried to help me out there."

"I can't hold your hand. I can't be your guardian angel. Any improvement or adjustment has to come from within you. We can explore choices and alternatives to your thoughts, feelings, and behaviors, but I won't tell you what to do or say unless I think you have no insight to whatever situation is presenting itself to you."

"I don't want to stay back at this place for long."

"You were helpful to some other people for a while out there, according to Jack. How did that make you feel?"

"Good. It was good to help some of the older people, especially."

"How about if you come to group therapy tomorrow and talk all about your experience living out there in a different community than downtown here, especially the positive aspects of it? I'm sure you realize that some of the patients here are afraid to get out because they've been here a long time."

"OK. I'd like that. It is better out there. You have more freedom."

Warren did what Greg suggested the next day in group therapy, and the group went very well. A couple of patients even thanked him for his comments and insights. He came into Greg's office a few days later and said, "It was nice to be appreciated by a few people in group the other day. There were no smart-ass comments about how I was lying, or I didn't know what I was talking about."

"Sounds like you're feeling good about yourself. Do you want to talk more about what happened that started you going downhill out in the community?"

"I was under a lot of pressure. A couple of former patients were going around telling people in the day treatment program not to trust me because I was a liar and a thief. My landlady told me I 'didn't fit in' with the people at the boarding house. I found out a few days ago from Lance that somebody told her I was selling drugs."

"Did you actually do drugs or sell drugs out there?"

"I bought and sold some medications because I needed the money, but not any street drugs. I didn't sell any meds to people in the boarding house, just a couple of former patients. The reason I did it was because I did some gambling – playing cards with some guys I met at a bar. I lost more than I won. The time I did have a good winning night, I met a girl inside that bar, bought her a drink, and she agreed to go out with me on a date the next night. I'll admit I was feeling no pain. I was supposed to meet her outside the bar and go to a movie with her. But she stood me up, and I was angry when I went back to the boarding house. That's when my landlady told me she wanted to throw me out. I just snapped and took the pills on impulse."

"So, I hope you admit that you did several self-destructive behaviors that led to your being hospitalized again."

"Yeah. Selling the meds, playing cards for money, drinking, swallowing the pills instead of calling somebody. I never should have asked that girl out."

"Well, you can't change what happened. What do you think you could have done differently? You just said calling somebody for help was one thing."

"I should have tried to look for a part-time job, but it's hard because it's a smaller town there than it is here. I got to stay away from drinking, if I can. Don't try to meet girls when you're high or drunk – she probably laughed at me. I hope I'm not getting a bad reputation out there."

"First of all, when you start to get angry with people in the day treatment program, or anywhere else, think before you act or respond. Think about how much you value their opinion. Be honest with people and be honest with yourself. It's OK to say what you feel, but there's a right way and wrong way to do that. Again, we've talked a lot in group therapy in the past year or so about being assertive instead of aggressive or non-assertive. You can do it. Tell yourself you can make it out there."

Greg saw Warren again for another session on Tuesday. This was focused more on "positives" – gains he had actually made in the past two years.

"Warren, you've come a long way in the almost two years since I've known you. Your appearance is cleaner. You're dressing appropriately. I haven't heard any reports of grandiosities or threats this admission. You're respecting yourself. Hopefully, you're respecting others, too. Good job."

"I want to make more changes. I want to be called "Ernie" when I get out of the hospital."

"Ernie?"

"Yeah. That's my middle name. Warren is my hospital name."

"OK. Make sure you tell Vance and Jack that. How will people at the clinic and ex-patients out there respond to that?"

"I don't care. I'll just tell everyone out of the hospital that Ernie is my name now, and it's legal, so deal with it. Another thing – I have to talk to Dr. Presley about my meds."

"Is there a problem?"

"Yeah. I want him to switch me to a shot of Prolixin every two weeks. I won't overdose on any pills that way."

"He's leaving at 4 o'clock, so you better see him soon."

"I will. Before I leave here, there's one more thing. I got to get a job. I want to work part-time, and my finances are in bad shape right now. I'm poor."

"You need to see Dolph and maybe Vance to set you up with Voc. Rehab. out there. You're going back to the same town, I assume."

"Yeah. I think I'm ready to get out of here again."

"I agree. I'll bring it up in team meeting tomorrow."

The team agreed that Warren could be discharged soon. However, he had to stay in the hospital for about another week because he needed to get a new living situation. Dolph and Vance took care of that quickly. Jack and the clinic staff could provide him with much support, and an older patient with whom he was friendly was going to the same placement situation. Warren was discharged on October 25th.

"He'll be back by Christmas," some nurses and aides said.

Chapter 12:
JUST WHEN YOU THINK HE IS OUT
FOR GOOD

For the rest of the fall, Warren did well at his new group home, helping with chores and going to the clinic's day treatment program regularly, as well as weekly therapy sessions with Jack. He secured part-time work stocking shelves at a local department store for the Christmas season. Although this lasted only four weeks (15 hours a week), it brought in some extra money along with his monthly SSI check, most of which went for room and board at the group home. There were a couple of ex-patients from the state hospital with whom he hung around, and he seemed generally happy.

Things changed right at the start of the new year, however. He and one of his ex-patient friends who he met at the clinic started drinking a couple of beers at a local bar most days after the day treatment sessions were over. Two beers started turning into three, then four, then with a shot of bourbon after the last beer. He came back to the group home drunk and missed dinner several times, which led to arguments with the people in charge. He would show up at the clinic with a hangover and in an irritable mood. A few times he had loud outbursts toward the activity leaders and left the groups to go out in back of the clinic and smoke for a while in the sub-zero weather. Jack cancelled a committee meeting to have an emergency session with him late in the day on January 19th.

Jack bluntly said to him, "Warren, you're going downhill. You're self-destructing again. If you and Dick keep getting drunk every day after the clinic closes, you're risking getting committed to the state hospital again. I don't want to see that happen, and nobody at the clinic does, either."

"I finally have some freedom to do what I want to do   do what a lot of other guys do after work. Dick is my best friend right now. We're trying to live normally, like most people would."

"Going to bars and getting smashed several times a week is not what most normal people do."

Warren cut him off, "I wasn't getting drunk – maybe once – people go to the Ramada Inn for happy hour. Happy hour food is better than where I live most of the time. Hey, I 'm not getting into any trouble. The cops aren't stopping me or coming to the house. Besides, I'm starting to get sick of the clinic. Some of the patients in the groups should be in the state hospital – they bother me. I don't have any friends at this place where I live, either."

"The reports I've heard this week from people at the group home and the clinic are that you're getting out of control again – angry outbursts. Yeah, you have more freedom than what you had at the hospital, but you're not handling it well. You're getting out of control."

"I'm not out of control. I just need to be away from people at the clinic and the group home as much as I can. Things were better when I was working. What have you and Vance heard from Voc. Rehab. lately? I thought I'd have a steady job by now, at least half-time. I've tried, but I can't find anything on my own."

"If you're drinking every day like you have been, that tells me you probably can't handle any kind of a job. Do you want start going to AA meetings?'

Warren cut Jack off again, "I don't want to go to AA! I don't need AA!"

"Then you need more things to do with your time. Stop drinking first, get some hobbies and interests - you used to like to draw, paint, even write. Everybody everywhere in life deals with rules. Everybody at one time or another deals with people they don't like, even jobs or supervisors they don't like."

The session continued with a discussion of Warren's frustration and anger about being "stuck" and independence not progressing for him as fast as he expected. Toward the end of the session, they discussed more positive things Warren had experienced compared to when he was in the state hospital. He also brought up how much he missed Midge and he had not met anyone to replace her. At the end of the session, Warren agreed to stop drinking. His friend Dick, coincidentally, decided to stop drinking also.

About a month later, after an argument over the food in the group home, Warren went out, got drunk, and superficially cut his left wrist. He was admitted to the local general hospital, but instead of being sent back to the state hospital, Jack helped get his admission lessened to two days. Warren was very thankful, and he said he was going to start keeping a diary as well as contacting Jack or calling the hospital's crisis line whenever he was feeling angry or depressed. There was a change in his medication, however, from Prolixin IM to Mellaril and Tofranil by a hospital psychiatrist.

Things went slightly better for him for the next two months. He was doing some volunteer work at a kitchen in a nursing home in addition to cooperating with the day treatment program, but he periodically called the crisis line and went to the emergency room a couple of times - once because he thought he was having seizures, and another time because he took a slight overdose of his medications, hoping it would help him sleep. Jack was called by the ER staff both times and he convinced them that Warren didn't need to be admitted.

Warren started drinking again by the end of April. He started withdrawing from people at the clinic, quit volunteering, and was thrown out of a local bar one night for being drunk and disorderly. Fortunately, he shunned attempts by bar patrons that night, and a few days later, to get back into gambling when they saw him on the street. After Jack moved to Florida on April 30th, Warren started going to a liquor store and he bought pints of vodka almost every day. Over a 12-day period, he began drinking a pint every night, then a pint most late afternoons, then a pint every morning. He was hospitalized on May 12th at the local hospital after he was found passed out behind the group home while drinking a fifth of vodka. Two days later he was reportedly verbally hostile and uncooperative to the ward staff at the general hospital, and he was re-admitted to the state hospital on May 14th. Immediately he became belligerent, yelled and took a swing at Joan White as soon as he got to the unit (in reply to her big sarcastic smile), and he was sent to Maximum Security. Greg met with him that Friday afternoon when he came back to the unit.

"Warren, I just read your chart. Apparently after six months of being out there, you started getting drunk all the time. I want to hear it from you exactly what happened."

"I de-gressed."

"You mean you regressed."

"Regressed, de-gressed – it's the same thing."

"Let's start with after you got out of here in October."

"I'll tell you the whole story. I did some volunteer work at a nursing home for a couple of hours a few days a week, and I went to the clinic programs. Around Christmas Jack told me this was the best he'd ever seen me, and a couple of people who used to be patients here said I looked a lot better than I did years ago. I went to the hospital one night in the winter because I got drunk and I thought I was having seizures, but they didn't admit me. They said I cut my wrist, but I don't remember how that happened. The psychiatrist at the clinic took me off the Prolixin and gave me pills – Mellaril and Tofranil – but I still couldn't sleep well at all. I left the job at the nursing home and became a Red Cross volunteer for a few weeks, but I quit when I started seeing a girl named Pam – I met her at a health food store in town. That didn't last long – I kept complaining about how my right foot and my back started hurting me more, and she got tired of hearing that, I think. Then a Voc. Rehab. counselor talked to me about plans for me to go to college and take some courses, but that fell through. I was bummed out and took a bunch of meds, but the hospital didn't admit me again. They called Jack and I wound up getting sent home. I got elected as the Day Treatment Club President, but to celebrate, I went out to a bar and got drunk.

"Then I started going to the same bar, mostly with Dick, for the next two weeks every night until they threw me out and told me not to come back. I started going to AA meetings every day after the first week, but I was hung over every meeting. I got a sponsor, but I didn't trust him. Instead, I started drinking beer – I thought that would be better than Harvey Wallbangers. I started getting depressed, especially when Jack moved to Florida. He told me he was moving a few weeks earlier and the last few times I saw him. I didn't believe he would actually leave and go so far away. I went for a walk along the railroad tracks and found most of a fifth of coffee brandy, so I drank it. That's when I started getting drunk all the time, buying vodka. I went to the clinic one day and I told them my head felt like a broken watermelon. The psychiatrist changed my meds back to Prolixin shots and told me that if I didn't stop drinking, I'd be dead by the end of the year. Later that day I passed out in the backyard of the group home after I drank a fifth of vodka. When I came to, I was in the hospital and started feeling paranoid – like everybody was talking about me. That's when I wound up here. I wanted to hit Joan White and I cursed at her."

"You had a hard time sustaining any success you had out there. What's your feeling about being back here now?"

"I don't want to stay here long. I signed a Voluntary when I came in. I need a rest from everything. I have got to stop drinking. I did better when I was taking the Prolixin, having Jack around, and going to the clinic groups. I need some things to keep me busy. I need some kind of a job or do volunteering again."

"When you get out of here, do you want to go back there or somewhere else?"

"I want to try to make it there again. It's a good town and the clinic and hospital people have been good."

"Warren, I'll do my best to advocate for you getting back out of here soon. I'll bring it up in team meeting Monday. But ultimately Dr. Presley has to agree to discharge you. Also, Dolph and Vance and a couple of former hospital employees who work at that clinic probably ought to be involved in a discharge plan for you that would include lots of support. It's your choice, but it would help if you gave AA another try and got a sponsor."

"I'll just hang around the unit and my room this weekend."

There was a long discussion about Warren in team meeting on the 22nd. Vance was present, as was Warren for the first 20 minutes of the meeting. Warren appeared to be rational and remorseful – no anger, no grandiosity, no blaming others for his admission. Dr. Presley was impressed with Warren's mental status, saying, "This is the best I've ever seen Warren. Maybe we should try to get him out of here very soon. Let's see how he does through the week."

Dolph immediately started making plans, along with some help from Vance, to get a placement and a support system lined up for Warren. By Friday, plans were in place for him to be discharged by the end of the month.

Warren did very well all week on the unit and Dr. Presley gave him off grounds privileges "as a test" for Memorial Day weekend, despite objections from some nursing staff. If Warren could handle the privilege level well with no incidents or breaking any rules, he could be discharged on Tuesday. Greg saw Warren in his office on Friday morning.

"Warren, you look good now, you say you're feeling good, and almost all of the staff thinks you're ready to give it a go again out there."

"I don't want to come back here again."

"I hope you don't. But, God forbid, in case that does happen, I hope you stay out longer and if there is a next time, I hope it's only for a few days. Part of deinstitutionalization sometimes means that there's what we call a 'revolving door.' What I mean by that – and I know you've seen this with other people here – is that sometimes patients come in and out of this place, but it's not necessarily at all a failure. I'm not talking about people who have been here a lot of times who get strung out on drugs come in for the winter because they have no place to go or to get out of going to jail. Instead, there are people who have been here in the past for months or years who know, at least deep down within themselves, that they need help when they come back here. The longer people stay out between admissions here and the shorter they stay when they come back, many times they don't come back at all. Support out there sure helps – therapists, day treatment programs, medications, friends and acquaintances, as well as knowing what to do with your time, and AA or NA if it's needed. If you got these things, you'll handle stress better."

"I got to keep it going. I just got to believe in myself after all these years here."

"Did Jack ever teach you any relaxation exercises?"

"Yeah. He gave me a paper on that stuff. I have it somewhere. All about breathing and tightening and relaxing muscles. Sometimes in a group at the clinic they do a little of that."

"Practice that every day, especially every time you feel like you're getting stressed out. Also, talk to yourself mentally to stay calm."

"What? How?"

"When you're getting upset or getting depressed, tell yourself, 'This is getting me upset. I'm not gonna let this get me upset. If I get upset, I'll get mad, or start drinking, or do something destructive and this will get me going downhill again. I'll do some relaxation exercises now. I'll call somebody after that if I have to.' Can you try that?"

"At this point, I'll try anything that'll keep me out of the bughouse."

"Practice that stuff this weekend. Good luck. Don't do anything impulsive that gets you in trouble. I hope you leave here Tuesday morning."

Warren had a good weekend and was discharged Tuesday morning.

Chapter 13:
STRUGGLING IN SOCIETY

Warren went to a residential program Greg helped start up about two years before – The Lodge – in the same town where he had been placed the last two times he was discharged from the hospital. The Lodge originally had nine patients move out of the hospital as a group to a house a year earlier. A couple of these ex-patients were re-admitted to the hospital, but the rest, aside from one who had a brief re-admission, made it out successfully. At the time the program started, the group didn't want Warren and he didn't want them. However, their attitude changed in May, 1978 and he was happy to be placed there. Lenny, a mental health worker at the hospital who was on loan to the mental health clinic in that town, had an office in the Lodge. He had been the major day-to-day contact with the residents from the beginning of the program, and he worked at The Lodge at a 9 to 5 job during the week. The residents either had jobs at the local sheltered workshop or did volunteer work in the community. Lenny was more of a non-directive "guide," encouraging the residents to self-govern. Although he was incredibly supportive toward every member of the group, he only made decisions for them when it was absolutely necessary. Vance, the hospital liaison social worker at the clinic, saw Warren for individual therapy sessions every week. Still, some people who worked at the hospital and also a few staff members at the clinic thought that Warren would be back in the state hospital in a matter of several months.

The summer of 1978 went generally very well for Warren, with one brief exception. One hot early evening at the end of July he and another Lodge member took a walk over to the Ramada Inn for happy hour to drag out one beer and eat the free bar food. They kept talking with a few of the patrons and one beer turned into four. Warren started getting loud and a little grandiose, but in a laughing, joking way. The guy he was with, Dave, said, "We better get out of here – we're getting drunk, and the price of beer is going up, anyway."

Warren replied, "I'm having a good time here, but you're right."

The next morning, he had a wicked hangover and had to go to the local hospital's emergency room because he took several Tylenol, Mellaril, and Cogentin trying to short-cut the hangover. He was there for about three hours and returned to the Lodge. The group voted not to evict him but suggested that he should go to AA and get a sponsor (almost everyone in the Lodge knew about his drinking history). Warren started going to AA meetings regularly and had a sponsor that he liked. He also worked almost full-time at the sheltered workshop in town. He had some supportive friends at the Lodge. However, his right foot started bothering him more often through the early fall and he had surgery on it in November, resulting in a cast. He kept doing very well at the Lodge, the workshop, the sessions with Vance, and AA right through Christmas holidays.

But in January, Lenny left for a job in Maine and Warren started to go downhill. He quickly became more irritable and seclusive. He overdosed on some medications he had because he felt that he couldn't get rid of feeling anxious and depressed. He walked into the emergency room alone; Vance was called by ER personnel and Warren went back to his room in the Lodge program several hours later. That Saturday he swallowed some of his medications again, only this time he also broke into a female Lodge resident's room and ingested several Lithium tablets he found in her drawer. This time he spent two nights in the ICU at the local hospital, and they subsequently sent him back to the state hospital on a Voluntary admission. That afternoon, during the last week of the month, he walked into Greg's office accompanied by an evening shift aide (Warren was on a 1 to 1 status). He looked thin, but appropriately dressed. He stood in front of Greg's desk with a blank look on his face and spoke.

"You know why I'm back in the bughouse again, don't you?"

Greg, deciding to take an unconventional but slightly risky therapeutic approach, said, "Warren, I heard you made two suicide attempts in the past week – the one last weekend was serious. How many times have you REALLY tried to commit suicide?"

Warren loudly replied, "Six times!"

"You're not too good at it, are you? By that I mean that if you are religious at all – and I know you claimed you were Catholic – somebody up there (gesturing to the sky outside the window) doesn't want you to do that. I remember – and I know you remember this – that you were bragging in group therapy one day that you wanted to outlive your grandfather who was over 100 years old when he died. What happened to that motivation? Be honest with me."

Greg told the aide to wait outside the door. Warren bowed his head and after almost a minute started to sob softly. He said, "I don't know. I didn't think I was getting enough support. Lenny left and that hurt. Vance tried, but I can't see him every day. I got the impression that people at the hospital, or the clinic, or the crisis line thought, 'Oh no – not him again,' whenever I saw them or called. My job at the workshop wasn't paying me enough – they didn't want to keep me on full-time and I was clearing only

$25 a week. I broke up with a girlfriend I had for a while because she blew up to almost 200 pounds – that's 70 heavier than me. I met her at an AA meeting and a couple of weeks ago we both started drinking a lot. I feel like I'm hitting a dead end with everything."

"On the positive side, at least you agreed to come back here on a Voluntary. If you were committed on an Involuntary, it'd be harder for you to get out of here."

"I might be here for a little longer this time. I don't want to go back to where I was. I hear I have more friends from the hospital living downtown now. A few of the people at the Lodge were OK, but some others weren't. My AA sponsor got to be a pain in the ass, too."

"Another important thing for you to do is to contemplate what 'warning signals' you have within yourself when you feel things are starting to go downhill for you. Write them down, if you can."

"You know, I've kept kind of a diary the last couple of years off and on. I'll bring it in to show it to you sometime. Can I read that booklet you have on depression over there?"

"Sure – keep it. I'll see you in team meeting tomorrow. Then I'll be out of town for a couple of days after that, but let's meet again Monday afternoon at 1:30."

He agreed and left the office.

Warren was brought into team meeting the next morning and his treatment plan was done. After he left, a couple of the nurses worried that he would eventually kill himself within a few years. A couple of other staff felt he would be "revolving door" for the rest of his life, never staying out of the hospital for more than about a year at a time, at best. Greg, Dolph, and a social work graduate student were convinced that at some point he could stay out of the hospital and live a relatively stable life with the right support system.

"He's growing up in his late 20's with a lot of issues people have who are 8 to 10 years younger," the grad student said.

"You may be right. Read 'Passages' by Gail Sheehy," Greg added.

A discussion about whether to take Warren off suicide precautions ensued. The team was split on this; Dr. Presley had the final decision and he declared that Warren should stay on suicide precautions for now.

Warren came into Greg's office on Monday afternoon. It was a longer session than usual.

"I was disappointed that Dr. Presley didn't take me off suicide level until this morning," Warren said, as he limped in the door.

"If you put yourself in his position, what would you do?"

"He knows me better than that by now. I promised him that I wouldn't break any rules. Besides, I think I have a better understanding of depression now from that booklet you gave me."

"Well, in team meeting today nursing staff said you kept your word for the lat five days. You can cooperate, if you want to."

"It's not easy when you got someone sitting there like a prison guard. At least almost everybody they had shadowing me was one of the younger aides I liked. What's that chart you have on your wall there about what people need to stay out of the state hospital? Did you make it up yourself?"

"I did – back in August."

"I got most of those things."

"Let's go over them. Basic Survival Provisions – Food, clothing, and shelter. You have no problem getting the first two, but you need a place to live.

"Stable Mental Status – You need to control your impulses when you're under stress. I don't think you're crazy, but there are times you do crazy, self-defeating things. Write down your strengths and weaknesses honestly – you're at the age where most guys start knowing what they are.

You seem to be controlling your anger better more often, and you'd probably do better if you're in an AA group with a sponsor.

"Awareness Of Danger to Self/Others – You just got off suicide precautions. When you're under stress and you start to do something to hurt yourself or someone else, mentally yell to yourself, 'Stop!' Think of how you can better handle the situation. Anticipate the consequences of your behavior.

"Money - You have it in you to manage your finances OK, as long as you don't throw it away by drinking and gambling.

"Contacts With People – Think about whether or not you have five close friends or family members that you can be in touch with at any time, or who are willing to help you in some way – outside of the hospital, is what I mean. A support system.

"Structuring Time – I know that you want to get a full-time job someday, but it probably has to be with the right training and supervision. Also, think to yourself, 'Is most of my leisure time when I don't work or volunteer somewhere spent constructively? What hobbies or interests do I have?' Structuring time might be the most crucial factor for staying out of places like this.

"Transportation – This could be a tough one. I know you can go several blocks away without getting lost, and you could even walk a mile if you had to. Someday you might need a cane. There's no public transportation unless you live in a larger city, and cabs are expensive.

"Physical Health/ Hygiene – Enough said. We both know you've learned some hard lessons about that in all the years you were here. You're doing a lot better lately.

"Legal And Moral Norms Of Society – You're better about taking responsibility for behavior in recent years, but you did steal medications from people out there during your last two suicide attempts. You have a long history of breaking or bending rules wherever you've lived. It's amazing that you've never been arrested or spent any time in jail.

"Finally, Social Awareness – You're OK with that. You listen to the radio, watch TV, go to movies, dress more appropriately than you used to, and you usually have good manners. That could help lead to making acquaintances and friendships, especially if you get aware of current events, and information from newspapers and magazines."

As he looked at the chart, Warren responded, "I don't want to go back to the Lodge. I need another place to live. Any meds I take are supposed to keep me from going insane. Going to AA all depends if I get a sponsor I like. I need a job so I can make money. I really don't want to be on SSI or Welfare unless I really have to. I don't gamble anymore. I don't know if I ever had much of a support system. If I can't get a job, at least I'll try to volunteer someplace that might lead to a job. I don't want to use a cane. I want to try to learn to drive a car someday if my foot and leg can tolerate it, or at least I can ride a bike. I've been lucky about jail. I know the difference between right and wrong."

"The next big thing now is to get you out of here again in a few weeks or so. It'll take longer this time because you want to be discharged to a placement in this town. Dr. Presley has to agree to it, and Dolph has to find you a place with enough support that you won't be coming back here again and again. Warren, you're better off than when I first met you 3 years ago."

"There's a TV program on depression tonight and I want to watch it. I need dental work, and my cast comes off in a few weeks. I really should to go to AA again, go to work, and feel better about myself. Can I have a sheet of paper so I can write down these 10 commandments you got up there on the wall?"

"Sure. Let's meet again Friday at 3. I'll see you in group on Wednesday."

Chapter 14.

A ONE MONTH STAY THIS TIME – OR LONGER?

Friday's session with Warren started with him saying that it was hard for him to express his feelings assertively because of the "old habit I have of holding things in until I can't make them go away. Other times I fly off the handle. It's a learning process for me."

"You're getting better self-insight. One of the best things you can try, in controlling your emotions, is to say to yourself, 'STOP! Think before I act!' Some people even put a rubber band around one of their wrists and snap it to keep their minds from 'snapping.' Like I've been saying, it's all about anticipating consequences of behavior."

"It's all about who I trust. I trust you. I trust Dolph. I trust Vance. I hope I can trust an AA sponsor. I did trust a couple of people at the Lodge.

Maybe one activity person at the clinic. Almost nobody else. I don't want to go back to the Lodge or that town again. I want to make a new start here."

"By here, do you mean the hospital?"

"No. Downtown. I know where everything is and I have some friends living here. I know there's a chance I'd come back to this place some more, but if that happened, I hope it'd be only for a few days at a time."

"Here's what came down in team meeting today when your name came up. Dr. Presley decided that he will refuse to discharge you to live independently. The majority of team members also feel that way given your track record. Dolph said placements in this town are hard to find right now. The team's opinion is that you'd be better off in a small, supervised place with some kind of work, or a workshop component involved, along with at least a weekly or day treatment follow-up at the mental health clinic downtown."

"That's OK. I'll stay here until something like that came up, if I can have off-grounds privileges and I'd just have to check in for breakfast, dinner, and meds. My secret hiding place in another building and the stuff I had there was gone last year, but I'll find another place in another empty building. I could get a patient payroll job or go to a few groups. But if it's late at night and I'm feeling depressed, I need somebody to talk to (his voice started rising). When I called the crisis line the last couple of times when I was living at the Lodge, they didn't listen! They told me to go to the hospital! I thought they didn't want to deal with me, so I ODed. That proved to all those people that I needed help but going into the hospital could have been avoided if they listened to me."

Greg was tempted to tell him directly that he had to take responsibility for his behavior, but he felt that might have been untherapeutic and Warren probably would have stormed out of the office angrily. Instead, he paused for about 10 seconds and responded, "Well I hope people who provide crisis intervention here will listen to you more attentively."

"There are a couple of aides on the night shift I might be able to talk to, but then they'd write things up in my chart and the nurses would blow it all out of proportion. Anyway, if I'm out of here I'd have to call the crisis line about 3 or 4 times a week, even if it's just to say to them that it's a minor, not a major problem. When I was out, I had periods where I got bored and started getting drunk. Here's what I really need: I need to work either three full days a week or four to five part-time days a week. I need to go to AA every day. I need to go to the clinic in town for a couple hours a week. The rest of the time I need to do cooking, reading mysteries, playing pool, watching TV, listening to the radio, or going to movies."

"Sounds like you're on the right track about what to do with your time. About playing pool downtown – you're not 'Big Jim Walker,' or 'Bad, Bad Leroy Brown,' are you?" They both laughed.

Greg then said, "Getting back to expressing your feelings, and what happens with them, I want to show you something called the 'Gerson Grid.' You can almost do your own treatment plan with this technique. This is something I learned several years ago from a psychologist named Dr Paul Gerson who's in Worcester. Here's a sheet of blank paper. Better yet, I'll write out this diagram for you."

Greg drew a large grid, with "Thoughts – Feelings – Behaviors," horizontally across the top of the page, and "Problems – Strengths - Goals – Pitfalls," vertically down the left side. He then drew horizontal lines between them. He told Warren to note the things he "has and wants," "has and does not want," "does not have and wants," and "does not have and does not want."

Warren said, "Jeez, this is complicated. You don't do this with everybody, do you?"

"No, but I think this might be helpful for you to try. You wouldn't've been ready for this last year. Start with "Thoughts" and go down the column and write one or two of the things that you think most concern you. Then do the same thing for the "Feelings" and "Behaviors." Look at each space and write in your responses for each part of the grid, and we can discuss them."

Warren said, dismissively, "This is a pain in the ass. I don't want to do this."

Greg responded, "Do it on your own time in the next couple of days before our next session, over the weekend. Just give it a try and see what you can come up with."

"Is this to make you look good?"

"It can be helpful to you in making YOU look good, in terms of what you need to do to improve your life while you're here and when you get out of here."

"I can't promise I'll do this right."

"Please try it, and see what you come up with. I'll see you on Monday. Vance will be here on Tuesday and he might want to see you."

I'll tell Vance I don't want to go back there. I want a placement in this town."

On Monday, Warren came into Greg's office and Greg immediately asked, "Did you do your homework?"

"I started it, but the 'thoughts, feelings, and behaviors' thing about the 'problems' can keep changing. I need about 4 sheets of paper to do this thing, anyway.

He gave Greg a sheet with a "Problem" listed as, "Staying out of this place for good." For "Thoughts" he wrote, "I got to get out of here before I turn into one of those old zombies downstairs (on the geriatric ward)." For "Feelings" he jotted down, "I'm sick – sick of Joan White, Cindy defending her, and the older aides who have it in for me." For "Behaviors" he put, "I need to find a place and a job downtown myself, if Vance and Dolph can't do it."

"Well, that's a start, "Greg commented.

"Don't you think that I've improved in the past few years?"

Greg replied, "I thought about that this morning. Here's some letters you wrote a few years ago. Read 'em."

Warren read four of them out loud and started laughing. He smiled and said, "I'm still Sir Warren to these people – for me, at least, that's self-respect. And I'll always be Midge's Irish, even though she's out of my life."

Vance came to the hospital on Thursday. He and Greg saw Warren together. Warren had a new cast put on his foot that morning and he was using a walker. Vance remarked, as Warren came into Greg's office, "You sound like the ghost of Jacob Marley with that clanking sound."

"The Ghost of Christmas Future was the one Scrooge was afraid of the most. A lot of times I fear the future most."

Greg asked, "So you fear the future most because…?"

"When I get down on myself, even though I try not to show it. When I think maybe nothing good is gonna happen for me. When I think I'll never make it out of here forever."

Vance said, "They changed their mind at the Lodge. They want you back. Your friend Dick came back there – he was like a big brother to you."

"No, I'm not going back there. I'm better off here in this town."

"Think it over until I come back next week, Warren," Vance replied.

"I got to be here for at least another couple of weeks until the cast comes off. Dr. Pratt over at the M&S building wants me to stay here until at least then, and I will. He kept me from being a total cripple before."

Vance said, "OK, if that's what you want. I talked to Dr. Presley a little while ago and he'll keep you on suicide precautions for the rest of the week."

"What? He told me just before I came in here that I could probably start at the workshop on Friday if they have a slot for me."

Greg said, 'I agree with that, Vance. He's been a model patient this admission so far."

Vance smiled and said, "Keep up the good work, Warren."

At the end of the session, Vance and Greg went across the hall to Dolph's office to talk briefly about what transpired during the session. Dolph concluded, "If Warren insists on living downtown, I think it'll be at least until the end of the month, if not longer, until he gets out of here. There just aren't any placement opportunities open right now, for where he wants to be."

Dr. Presley took Warren off suicide precautions on the 19th, after the staff discussed his progress in team meeting, but insisted that he would not discharge Warren unless a closely supervised placement could be found. Warren's cast came off two days later, and he started at the workshop the next day. He was granted off grounds privileges the day after that, and his plan for most days was to come back to the unit only for meals and curfew in the evenings. During snowstorms and icy conditions, he most likely would stay in his room. That Saturday he discovered another hiding place, similar to the one he had a few years earlier, in an unused building that closed two years earlier. Warren carefully climbed through an unlocked first floor window and eventually established this as an occasional "weekend retreat" for a few hours at a time (especially on milder winter days), again with a cooler, a blow-up mattress, some food, beverages, and some magazines.

He came to see Greg late in the day on the 26th. During this session, he brought in his diary from August, 1977 to October, 1978. He read parts of it to Greg. Warren described the summer of '77 as, "wanting not to slip back into hospital tendencies." When waiting to see Jack at the clinic, he noted that, "every second seems like a year; every minute seems like a century." He described the thrill of gambling, mainly playing cards with college kids in an alley in back of a bar. They never invited him to their dormitory. When he went to ask a girl out on a date, he described having, "butterflies in my stomach," and also feelings of "loneliness," and "inferiority," when a girl shot him down. Late at night that year he started hearing "the negative voices of Joan White and some evening shift aides." He became convinced that "drinking beer at night helps drive away the voices in spite of the meds." He bought a second-hand bike and was able to ride it around town, saying, "It hurts a little, but it's better than walking."

Other random thoughts he vocalized:

"Jeez, money goes fast!"

"Things go better for me when I write down my feelings."

"I'm tired of people showing up late for appointments."

"I almost got into a fight coming out of a bar. It reminded me of one night in the late '60s when I was in restraints and I threw a bar of soap that hit an aide in the face, and he almost beat me into a coma, and he said he'd kill me if I told anybody."

"It was nice to hear from some folks at the clinic Christmas party that I looked better than they'd seen me in 10 years."

Regarding 1978, he said:

"After Jack left, I couldn't eat much and I couldn't sleep much."

"I got an ambulance bill for the time I went to the hospital in April – I sure as hell can't pay that!"

"I'm trying to get an apartment with Dave (a former state hospital patient), but nobody will rent to us."

In May:" Drinking for me is the best way to cope with life – at the Lodge there are a couple of social drinkers, but a few heavy drinkers."

Just before his admission in May: "I've only had five meals in the last five days. I'm hung over every day. I'm gonna try to start drinking black coffee and try to cut back on alcohol."

"People at the hospital and the Lodge are talking about me a lot – I know they are."

That fall: "My foot's hurting a lot. I'm taking a lot more meds than I should to ease the pain."

"AA meetings are good lately – I told my story at the last meeting and nobody put me down."

Greg emphasized to him, "You've been fighting through a lot of obstacles and self-destructive stuff, but you keep making comebacks."

"I've decided it's not worth it to try to kill myself when I need help. I've come a long way since I first tried to get out of this place. But I still think about Midge. I'd really want to see her again. We're both probably much better than we used to be."

"You are better than you were when you were with Midge and you can get out of here again. I don't know if Dolph told you yet, but there's more good news for you – he got you an appointment for an interview at Second Chance House downtown for the afternoon of the 28th. He's probably waiting to talk to you about it after you see me today. If that doesn't work out, I'm sure he'll keep looking for other placement possibilities."

"No, I didn't know that," Warren said, excitedly. "I want to see him, now."

Dolph wasn't in, but a note on his door indicated that he'd be back in about 20 minutes. For the rest of the session, they talked about assertiveness vs. non- assertiveness vs. aggressiveness in an interview situation. Greg tried to do some role playing with him, regarding the interview. Warren did well, but Greg told him to be prepared for disappointment if the placement didn't come through. Warren indicated that he would be "ready for that possibility", and should that occur, he promised he would not do anything self- destructive. He went to see Dolph, who told him that the interview was postponed, but they wanted Warren next week to have dinner there with some residents and staff during the first week of March.

On the 27th, Warren finally got the cast off. He still had some trouble walking, and even bending his knee, but Dr. Pratt told him that by mid-April, the healing process should go much better for him.

Chapter 15:
STUCK

Warren began March by joining an alcohol/drug abuse day treatment group on the hospital grounds. After discussing this in team meeting the day before, it was suggested that this program would require a two day per week commitment from him, and Warren readily agreed. It was also decided in team meeting, and approved by Dr. Presley, that Warren could get more dental work done, as well as an appointment to see an ophthalmologist as he recently started complaining of becoming nearsighted. There was some discussion among staff in the meeting regarding whether or not any nearsightedness or blurry vision could be due to side effects of Prolixin, but Dr. Presley said, "Let the ophthalmologist decide." Dolph stated that Medicaid would pay for it. Warren had said, at a team meeting a few weeks earlier, that he wanted to "get everything checked out and done (regarding any physical issues)" before he got out of the hospital this time.

He was still walking with a cane when Greg saw him briefly on March 6th.

"How was dinner at Second Chance House last night?"

He smiled and replied, "It went real good. The place and the people were nice. Nobody made any snide remarks to me. They want me for an interview there on Friday. I'm gonna get out of here for good and outlive my grandfather."

"I'll see you later in the day on Friday. Come by about 3 o'clock."

"I'll tell you all about it."

Warren didn't show up to see Greg that Friday afternoon. Ward staff said he was asleep in his room, and he didn't want anyone to bother him. He asked Shari, the charge nurse, to tell Greg he'd see him on the 13th. Greg called Pat De Soto, the new Voc. Rehab. counselor assigned to the unit and asked him what happened with Warren's interview at the halfway house.

"There were 6 people in the interview, one was Dr. O'Dell – she's a psychologist who is a consultant to the same clinic Warren was at last year."

"Oh, no," Greg said. "He didn't expect that many people interviewing him. And Dr. O'Dell has a reputation for being arrogant and condescending." Greg didn't mention that Jack Orvis had several run-ins with her when he was a graduate student two years ago.

"I was there. It actually went fairly well. Warren seemed pleased with the attention at first, but after a little while Dr. O'Dell started questioning his future commitment to the group of residents there, based on his history. Warren started to say that he was 'just asking for a chance,' but then he seemed to bite his tongue and he stayed silent. Unfortunately, Sam (Director of the Program) reluctantly agreed, after a brief verbal exchange with her."

Greg thought, "Why that bitch! Jack was right."

Pat continued, "Looks like we may have to find another placement for him."

"Thanks, Pat. Talk to Dolph about this. Maybe we can work something out with Sam and do an 'end run' around Dr. O'Dell."

"Well, it's true Sam makes the final decision, not Dr. O'Dell."

Warren couldn't see Greg on the 13th because he was getting dental work done. Greg was working until 9 p.m. that day. He and Warren crossed paths as Greg was going out to dinner, and Warren said, "I just want to go to bed for a while. I'll stop in and see you after your group tonight, or before you go home."

At 8:15 Warren came into Greg's office.

Greg said, "Hey, I got some good news for you, Warren. Dolph talked to Pat De Soto today. Pat called Sam and he told Pat that you're still under consideration for living there. But Pat also said that State Voc. Rehab. won't provide any training funds for you unless you live in a structured setting. I don't know if they call a halfway house a structured setting or not."

"Nah. That's my 3rd choice now. I want to live at the YMCA downtown, but I'll go to the Morse Center (a live-in vocational program in a city 20 miles away) if they pay my rent in the live-in program there. My friend David is there now."

"You've been doing your research lately."

"Well, Dolph has helped. I wouldn't put the halfway house totally out of the question if they want me, though. I just don't want to be trapped here too long. I can't understand why they rejected me last week, but you say now they'll reconsider me. Did you hear when they'll interview me again? I hope it's tomorrow or Friday. I hope that psychologist won't be there."

"Whoa, Warren! You should know by now that things don't necessarily work that fast in this system."

"Damn! I was so sure they'd accept me that I went downtown and told the Social Security office to forward my check there."

"You didn't tell Dolph about this? They'd have to contact him for a discharge date."

"No, I forgot. Yesterday he told me about two other places in the state that have openings, but I don't want to go to either one of them."

He talked briefly about the interview last week, and Greg complimented him about acting assertively and handling his emotions well. "Three years ago, you would've screamed, cursed at them, given them the finger, and stormed out of there. How you handled yourself with your thoughts, feelings, and behavior is probably why Sam is willing to interview you again."

"Things went OK at the dinner with the residents, too. I didn't know anyone there, although I used to see one guy around at another building here a couple of years ago."

"You still have to think before you act, though. Any time you have to deal with finances as long as you're here, let Dolph or whoever your social worker is, handle it. Going to the Social Security office and trying to convince them to forward your check there was really impulsive. It's amazing they didn't immediately question that and call here to confirm."

"I wanted to get everything in place."

"It's like driving when you see a caution light turn red and hoping another car doesn't slam into you. Think about that. I'll leave you with that thought because I have to go. I'll see you Friday afternoon around 3, after I meet with Dolph and Vance."

"I'll be around."

Vance came to the hospital on Friday. He, Greg, and Dolph had a phone conversation with Johnny Sudakis, Director of the State Voc. Rehab. Apparently, the halfway house staff, influenced by Dr. O'Dell, heavily weighed old reports they had about Warren from two to three years earlier in their decision to reject him. Johnny said, "They were wary of his history of suicide attempts and periods of heavy drinking. Dr. O'Dell even said that one evening last summer that she was with friends at a happy hour at the Ramada Inn and she noticed him with a ragged looking guy at the bar, and he staggered out of there."

"He walks with a staggered gait and maybe he wasn't drunk at all - just there for one beer and getting some decent food to eat," Greg said.

Johnny brushed off that comment and said, "Anyway, most places have a built-in workshop or work training program 16 to 20 hours a week. The concern is what he'll be doing for the rest of his time. There are real questions about how he 'd get along with co-workers and how he'd accept supervision."

"Warren would do well if he had supportive staff," Vance said.

Greg said, "He just started an on-grounds drug and alcohol abuse program here."

Dolph quickly interjected, "Warren will be going to physical therapy for a while, and he wants to go back to AA meetings and get a sponsor."

After some further discussion, they all agreed that Warren would need a transitional program (e.g., a workshop) leading to regular employment in the community, while living in a structured setting.

Johnny wanted to meet with them again to plan for one course of action and one alternative, but the soonest they could all get together would be on the 27th. Greg told Warren about the meeting later.

Warren grumpily said, "I really want to get out of here by the first few days of April."

"They want me to give an MMPI to you to fill out. Do you know what that is?"

"Yeah, I've done those things a couple times before. The stupid thing takes forever. About five or six years ago was the last time I had one. Nobody ever told me the results."

"I'll see you Monday afternoon and give the MMPI to you so you can fill it out in your room and slip it under my door when you're done. Then I'll mail it into the company and they will give me a print out of the scores and the interpretation."

"What? They can do that by computer?"

"Yeah – they just came out with that recently. The reason I'm doing it that way is because it'll be more unbiased and objective, and I've known you for three years. I'll have their report in about two weeks, hopefully."

That Tuesday morning the completed MMPI was slipped under Greg's door with a handwritten note from Warren stating that, "It took me two and a half hours."

Greg saw him briefly on Thursday, telling Warren that he had to go away through the end of next week. On the afternoon of the 26th, when Greg got back in the office, he got the computerized MMPI scores and report in the mail. The MMPI profile was typical of someone with psychotic signs, but getting better – i.e., no longer psychotic. He also left 10 items blank, so there was a slight possibility the test was invalid, but several of these were on the last 150 items, so the basic scales of the test were valid (at least in Greg's opinion).

Warren said, "I'm not crazy. I'll admit I did some crazy things in the past. The last 200 items my eyes were getting buggy, and I was getting tired. I had to take a break for a while. I want to get another eye exam, as long as I'm kept here. You know there are some days when my sense of taste and smell are better than anyone else's alive, and other days I can make them go away completely. I could be a drill sergeant in the Army. Maybe I should try to go into the Army."

"Now you're talking grandiose. You haven't said things like that in a long time. Anyway, back in the days of the draft you would've been 4-F."

"That's what they told me I was, but I was in here. That'd be one way to get out of the bughouse now."

"With the physical problems you've had do you think any branch of the service would take you?"

"I got a right to try."

"Why now, at 29 years old?"

"If I could take the stress of being in this place for all those years, basic training would be a piece of cake."

"And you would want to go into military service because…?"

"It'd give me a chance to make something of myself before I get too old."

"There are a lot less stressful ways to do that. Besides, if we can get you out of here and into a vocational training program, hopefully, it'd be comparable to some kind of specialized training you'd get in military service. This is what Dolph, Vance, and the Voc. Rehab. people are trying to do. We're meeting again tomorrow."

"I've been feeling like I don't have control over my life the way I want to lately. I probably shouldn't be here this long, but at least I'm getting myself taken care of physically and mentally before I get out. I mostly can come and go when I want. I get away a lot. I'm following the rules better. I can play the bughouse game better than ever. But it's not the same as being out of this place. Most of the people I've met here are out now."

"When you get into the next vocational training program, hopefully it'll last a long time and you can transition into a steady job. That seems like it's one of your long-term goals, and it'll keep you out of this place. The decision to change your life is up to you – remember how we talked about your thoughts, feelings and behaviors, and anticipating consequences of your behavior? That's what it's all about for you. You've been doing a real good job controlling the frustration of being in here longer than you expected."

"I've had trouble sticking with things and concentrating since I was a kid. I never really got disciplined. I try to work on it a lot more now. I thought I could get over easy on people by bragging and bullshitting. Every time I got money honestly, or dishonestly, I'd spend it as fast as I could because I'd be afraid I'd never see it again, or somebody would steal it from me. Same for anything I had in my secret hiding places on grounds. "

"Sounds like all the grandiose stuff you've come out with – at least since I've known you – and all the con schemes, lying you've been accused of, are just an attempt to build a façade of power in your mind, in some way."

"All to make me feel that I'm as good as anybody else."

"You can convince yourself you're as good a human being as anybody else without resorting to the b.s. Grandiosity is a cover-up for inferiority, but you can go beyond that. Everybody has setbacks and self-doubt, at times. Accomplishing goals will make you feel better about yourself. All the professional staff on the unit here would agree that you're far better off if you can get out of the hospital in the near future, which would be a start. Hopefully, with a supervised setting and vocational training for a regular job plus AA, you will either stay out a lot longer or maybe never come back here again."

"The big fear for me is that I might be stuck here for a long time."

"I hope not, but at least right now you have the freedom to come and go as you please as long as you cooperate with hospital rules and stay out of trouble off grounds. Keep trying to improve yourself while you're here, as best you can. I'll say it again – you're a lot better off than when I first met you."

The session ended, Warren left, and Greg thought, "It must be a bitch to grow up in the state hospital."

The meeting with Johnny Sudakis went well. Mike Speier, who represented the Morse Center, was also there. They talked about the possibility of Warren taking a bus to the city where Mike's program was located to train in a food service program if he were accepted. As they got out of the meeting, they crossed paths with Warren as they were about to leave the ward and informed him that his interview at the Morse Center was scheduled for April 6th.

Greg went back to his office with Warren and discussed the details of the meeting with him, saying, "It sounds like a good opportunity for you to stay out of this place if all goes well."

"Yeah, it sounds good, but I'll tell them I'll stay in the residential part for a few months and then I'll live on my own."

"If you say that, no place will accept you. The best-case scenario might be that you'd have to live in a supervised apartment with a room-mate, if the Morse Center would go for that. Someone affiliated with the Morse Center would have to live in the building, as a supervisor."

Warren responded in a surly tone, "Then if worst comes to worst, maybe I'll go back to where I was if Vance can arrange it. I don't need to be here anymore." He got up and left the office.

ROLLING WITH THE PUNCHES

On April 4th, Warren came into Greg's office just before 4 p.m. He said, "Since I'm probably leaving soon, I decided to go downtown to the Thrift Shop on Main St. and buy some clothes cheap. Jack told me once that he even bought clothes there. I think I got some real good deals. Wanna see what I got?"

"Sure, let's go to your room."

Warren opened a big plastic bag and took out a few pairs of pants, a few shirts, and a spring jacket. All of these were better quality than what he had been wearing.

"I'm impressed," Greg said. "Everything matches OK. Everything is appropriate – you won't look like a long-term state hospital patient. Just remember to keep up your hygiene."

"They all fit good, too. I saw Rob (an aide on the unit who was off that day) walking by the place as I was about to go in the door. I asked him to help me. He said he had a few minutes he could spend with me. By the way, I ordered a pair of low-cut orthopedic boots from a place in Pennsylvania last week for $20. They should get here any day now."

"That was nice of Rob to help you. I'll tell him that when I see him."

"The aides on the unit rarely bother me lately. They're mostly different people than a few years ago. "Most of the younger ones were always OK. I'm not around a lot, anyway."

"You will look good for your interview at the Moore Center a couple of days from now."

"I think I know what to expect. Vance is taking me there. I think it's in the afternoon."

"Good luck. I hope it comes through for you. It's a place where you can live and work, and to get a new start."

Greg saw Warren a week later.

Warren stated, "The interview went well, I think. I wouldn't mind being there. It's up to them if they want me."

"That'd be great, in my opinion, if you can go there. But what if they don't accept you? What alternatives do you have?"

"I want a room at the YMCA downtown. If I can save enough money, I'll try to move to Boston or Portland (Maine). I could get a full-time job."

"Think seriously about that. They are a lot bigger cities and you don't know anyone in either place, do you?"

"I have a cousin – a guy who lives somewhere around Portland."

"When is the last time you had any contact with him?"

"When I was about 14, but I could look him up in the phone book there."

"I'm taking a few days off for Easter weekend. I'm getting out of town tomorrow afternoon, but I want to see you to talk about this some more on Monday at 4 o'clock in my office."

In team meeting the next day, most of the staff thought Warren's plans were grandiose. Maureen, a social worker who went to graduate school in Boston, said that it was her belief that Warren could never survive there. Shari, the new day shift charge nurse on the unit who had worked in Maine, doubted that Warren would last long in Portland unless he had strict supervision, and that it would take a few years before he could live independently there. Vance related that he would not look for any placement for Warren in his area of the state unless all other alternatives were exhausted, but he added that he thought the Morse Center would make a decision regarding Warren next week. Dr. Presley said he was ready to discharge Warren if an appropriate placement was found, but he was skeptical of sending Warren downtown to the YMCA after what happened there a couple of years earlier.

On Monday Warren came into Greg's office and asked, "Have you heard anything?"

"No, but what I did hear from Jim (one of the aides on the ward) is that you said you don't need to go to AA except for once in a while. He also said you've been bragging that you could drink a couple of Miller Lite beers because it wasn't 'hard stuff.' Then he told me you want to change your name to 'Sir Ernest' again."

He laughed and said, "Jim blew that out of proportion. I'm getting tired of AA and I think a lot of people they have in those groups are jerks who are more drug addicts. I don't have a sponsor now. The guy went off the wagon and moved to Rhode Island. Besides, the alcohol content in Lite beer is hardly anything. What they say on TV is true – 'Less filling. Tastes Great.' I've been thinking about going by my middle name on and off for a long time."

"Well, I can see you going by Ernie when you get out of here, but 'Sir Ernest' is like back in your grandiose days. The idea of drinking any alcohol is self-destructive. You're so close to getting out of here, don't blow it. Remember how we talked about thinking before you act and consequences of your behavior?"

He loudly stated, "I want to get out of here. I have more freedom than I ever had in the bughouse, and I have my own space to get away from people again besides my room. I won't tell you or anyone where – but it's not the same as being out. Nobody tells me anything as soon as it happens – my grandmother died last week and I just heard about it last night. I was pissed off and went to Shari to complain about being kept in the dark. I was loud, but I stayed assertive. I wasn't aggressive. A few years ago, I would've torn up the place."

"It's really good that you have more emotional control than you used to. I'm so sorry to hear about your grandmother. Did you ask Dolph if you could go to the funeral?"

No. It was this morning at 9 o'clock. I was closer to my grandfather than her, anyway. I want to find out what happened about whether or not they'll take me at the Morse Center."

"I'll call Vance. If he's not around, I'll leave him a message."

Greg was in Dolph's office when Vance called the next day. Vance told Dolph that the Morse Center didn't want to take Warren into their residential program because they were worried about his ability to accept supervision.

Dolph said, "Let's talk to Warren right away. I noticed he was out on the unit playing pool a little while ago when I was coming back from charting some notes."

Greg said, "I'll interrupt the game and bring him back here now. He's not gonna like this."

When Dolph explained what Vance communicated to Warren about the Morse Center's decision, he immediately became upset.

He yelled, "That's bullshit! Do I have to sign out of here against medical advice?"

Greg responded, "Not a good move, Warren. You'd be asking Dr. Presley to find some way to keep you here involuntarily."

Dolph said, "Vance is meeting with Johnny Sudakis on Friday to see if there is any place in the state where can be discharged to. We've got to get you out of here soon because there is a possibility your SSI could be cut off."

"Yeah, well I'll raise hell and appeal with a lawyer if they try to do that to me!" He got up and left the office, quickly limping away.

The weather outside was beautiful on the 24th, so instead of seeing Warren in his office, Greg took a 40-minute walk with him on the spacious hospital grounds, avoiding most people.

Warren related that "Vance told me today that the meeting with Johnny Sudakis was cancelled because of an emergency at Johnny's home."

"That's too bad. Did he re-schedule it for some time soon?"

"I don't know, but Dolph saw me and he got me way up on the waiting list for a room downtown at the YMCA. He thinks I might be able to go there by the middle of next month. If that comes through, I'll ask Dr. Presley to discharge me, or I'll leave AMA. There's no reason to keep me here."

"You're keeping busy and staying out of trouble, from what staff tell me. What are you doing with your time when you go off grounds every day?"

"Oh, I stop in and see a couple of friends downtown who used to be patients here. I smoke a few cigarettes and have coffee with them. Or I look for a job, or else I hang out at the library."

"Be honest – you're not drinking are you?"

"No. I decided I don't like Miller Lite Beer and anything else will get me going downhill again. Pabst Blue Ribbon is tempting, though."

"Just think of what'll happen if you start drinking that stuff."

"I don't want to think about it because it depresses me. Maybe it's good that I stayed here this long this time. But I don't want to be cut off financially. I really want a job, anyway."

Chapter 17:

INSTITUTIONALIZED AGAIN?

In early May, two high functioning homeless hospital patients approached Dolph with the idea of getting a shared apartment with Warren, either downtown or in the town where the Morse Center was. Dolph and Greg brought up the idea in team meeting on May 8th. Vance was present and he related that there was another former patient (a long-time friend of Warren's) who was unhappy with his present living situation. Warren and one of the other patients, Jeff, happened to be available on the unit, and since his treatment plan review was due, Jeff was brought into the team meeting to discuss this plan further. Warren was also brought into the meeting.

Jeff asked, "Can the hospital give us each $300 for start-up money?"

Warren said, "It'd be in the form of loans."

Dolph responded that the chances of that would be "very slim."

Dr. Presley laughingly added, "and none."

Shari said, "First, it has to be defined exactly where you guys would live."

A few minutes later Warren left the meeting. Vance was called away to take a phone call.

When Vance returned, he announced, "I just got a call from Johnny Sudakis. The Morse Center is now reconsidering Warren to start in their supervised employment program, but somehow, we would have to furnish transportation. I hope to find out in the next couple of days whether or not they would accept Warren part-time or full-time."

Greg saw Warren briefly later in the day after Warren had talked with Dolph.

"Things are still up in the air, it seems," he said.

"Yeah. I think the odds I'll go to the Morse Center are 10-1. The odds I'll live with these guys are lower – about 5 to 1. The odds that I'll end up living downtown are probably better at 3 to 1."

"Don't look at the odds as much as what alternative plans you'll have if one thing or another falls through for you."

"If everything falls through, I'm thinking now, maybe I'll just stay here and do what I'm doing. I'm out of here during the day, but I'm showing up for meals, and staying in my room evenings. Nobody's bothered me for a long time now."

"I don't believe you said that - that you would be comfortable staying here. You know you have so much more freedom on the outside. You don't think you can handle responsibility for yourself out there if you have the right amount of support?"

"Yeah, but what I'm saying is that the less I'm around these people here, the better off I am as long as I do what they say – if they can find me. I still have my secret hiding place on grounds. Spring and summer are not that bad here if you know how to beat the system."

"Damn," Greg thought, "I hope he doesn't give up and get institutionalized after all these years of fighting it."

Greg saw Warren again on the 15th. There was a rumor that Warren was doing some part-time work at the library downtown, shelving books for an hour or two, one or two days a week. Greg confronted him about this.

Warren stated, 'I'll admit that I was volunteering there for a little while, but that's all I'll say to anybody. I got other news for you. Jeff's parents are taking him back and the other guys want to live alone. But the Morse Center accepted me for a 30-day trial and one of the aides who works in another building is gonna drive me and a girl who's a patient on his unit for four days a week there - paid training. I'll be working at the canteen there."

"Well, that's great news. Do they want you to live in their housing facilities?"

"No. Not yet, at least. They want me to stay in the hospital for another month. I told them that they could take their time. What I really need is some kind of steady job right now. I start there tomorrow."

"Do you really think you should have told them that they can 'take their time,' given how slow this process has been? They might think you don't really care about getting here."

"I never thought I'd say this, but I'm tired of fussing and fighting with anyone right now. Hey, I finally got the boots I sent away for – with the orthopedic fittings in them. They want me to wear my back brace when I'm at the Morse Center, but I always wear it when I'm working or walking downtown here, so that's no big deal."

"Good luck. I'll see you next week."

At the end of the month Dolph and Greg met with Warren. After the hospital Social Work department meeting earlier in the day, Dolph talked to Jan, the social worker who was working with the girl on her unit who was riding to the Morse Center with Warren. Jan mentioned that there might be a place for Warren to live right near there, but it would have to be a shared apartment.

Warren said, "Jeff changed his mind about living with his parents. I'll ask him if he wants to live with me there. If he doesn't, that's OK. I can live here and have almost as much freedom as I ever did. This is the most comfortable I've ever been here. I'm king of the patients on this unit now. I can wrap some of these new nurses and nursing students around my little finger – if I decide I want to be seen. I can get anything I want from most of the patients here, too – if I need anything."

Greg responded, "Now you're getting grandiose again."

"Let me know what happens with what Jan finds out," he said, smiling, as he got up and walked away.

Dolph said, "This is what happens when people like him who should be out of here stay too long."

Greg replied, "I know. I 've seen it a few times in the past few years since I've been here."

Sure enough, Warren's arrogance bordering on grandiosity got back to Joan White, who was reassigned back to Warren's ward at the end of the month, after she worked for a year on another ward. On June 4th, in team meeting one of the nurses said that Warren may have stolen an electric razor from a new patient over the weekend and had tried to sell it. In a statement written by another nurse (possibly Joan White) that the patient had signed, the patient said that Warren had possession of the razor and never returned it. The team consensus was that there should be further investigation before any discipline toward Warren might be taken. Dr. Presley agreed.

Greg saw Warren when he came back from the Morse Center late in the day. Warren angrily denied that he ever used the razor, and he declared that actually another patient on the ward must have taken it. He stated that he saw the razor lying next to a toilet stall and he had given it to one of the evening shift aides. Greg saw the aide at the nurses' station on his way out from work. The aide, after a brief discussion with Greg, admitted he "forgot" to give it back to the patient, didn't know how it ended up next to the toilet stall, and "forgot" to chart a note about the incident after Warren gave it to him, although what occurred had been passed along on the report to the next shift. The aide said that Joan White wanted Warren restricted to the ward. Dr. Presley decided not to restrict Warren's level of privileges, given Warren's acrimonious history with Joan White.

Greg crossed paths with Warren late the next day. Warren said, "I got to watch my back now that freakin' Joan White is here again. You're right. I got to get out of this place. But I love it when I beat that bitch in a power struggle."

Greg met with Warren on the 14th at the end of the work day. Warren said, "I think I'm doing real well there. I like the job training and I'm starting to make friends there. There's a younger girl there I like. My first evaluation is tomorrow. Dolph and Vance can't be there. Can you come?"

"I can't. I'm gonna be in a conference all day up north. But I'll call Judy, your team leader there, to see if she can send me a copy of the evaluation, or some kind of report about the meeting."

"I still want to go into an apartment with Jeff, but he's having second thoughts again. I think I'll go along with the Morse Center people wanting me to stay here for another month before they can get me into one of their places to live. But Dolph said he might be able to take me to look for an apartment around there if he gets the time."

"I really hope something comes through for you. You've been here way too long this time."

"I'm getting all my medical things taken care of. I got an appointment with an orthopedic surgeon here on the 26th for a checkup."

"I know you're not going to AA now, but you're not drinking again, are you?"

"No, but it's tempting. I have some Miller Lites at my hiding place, but it's not the same as real beer. Jeff says the first thing he's gonna do when he gets out of here is to get good and drunk. That's tempting for me. I have the urge to have a beer most days after work, but I haven't done it. I'll probably go back to AA if I ever get out of here. But I got to get a sponsor that I can trust."

"Get rid of the Miller Lites," Greg said, firmly.

Warren just smiled and replied, "I'll see you next week."

Chapter 18:
FINALLY: A LIGHT AT
THE END OF THE TUNNEL?

Judy Sanders wrote Warren's Morse Center evaluation during the first week of June, but the correspondence was addressed to Greg, and it didn't arrive at his desk until June 15th. However, the letter enclosed stated, "Dear Vance, We regret that you were not able to join us for an interpretation (of the evaluation)." She went on to describe Warren's Individual Client Service Plan and if there were any questions, please feel free to contact her.

Greg thought, "Why the hell couldn't I have been involved in this? I know him better than anybody. And why didn't Vance tell us about this? He must've got this last week." But Greg read on.

Judy's letter continued, "Warren wanted to be called 'Ernie,' while he was at the Morse Center. He has done well so far in the Food Services Program and has shown himself to be a well-motivated, conscientious worker, although he has shown a considerable need for assurance and is periodically overenthusiastic. It is recommended that he be accepted formally into Food Service training."

"That's good news," Greg thought.

However, her evaluation said that they would "stick to their original agreement that Ernie would need to be hospitalized for another month (a total of 60 days from the day he entered the Morse Center program) due to his past history of depression and suicidal tendencies when under stress. This will allow him to become fully acclimated to the program before he takes on the additional stress of living in the community."

Greg thought, "He's not gonna like that when he hears this."

Her evaluation continued, "Strengths: Verbal skills, grooming, motivation, conscientious, pleasant, cooperative, reading/math skills, attention to detail, punctual, work attitudes, desire to please."

Greg thought, "Wow! What a change from 3 ½ years ago."

"Weaknesses: Dealing with stress, impulse control, need for assurance, overenthusiastic, physical restrictions, consistent acceptance of supervision."

Greg thought, "Is this all by history?"

"Team Goal: To accept Ernie into Food Service Training with emphasis on skills leading to competitive employment:

Acquire the skills of canteen operator: (a) acquire the skills of a cafeteria attendant, including basic food preparation, and daily cleaning chores – by 7/79. (b) acquire skills of a cook's helper, including vegetable and fruit handling; also handling and serving fish, meat and poultry, doing some inventory control, and pertinent cleaning tasks – by 12/79. (c) begin to acquire the skills of a canteen operator, including serving sandwiches and canteen items, accepting cash, and knowing cash handling procedures, and taking ordering – by 6/80 to 12/80."

The plan went on to say that various staff would monitor his independent living skills, offer nursing services as needed, and monitor his involvement with the local mental health center – individual and group therapy. Also, there would be weekly meetings with his supervisor to discuss any concerns he would have with the program, as well as any staff feedback.

Finally, the plan stated, "The goals hinge on Ernie's being able to maintain an emotional equilibrium and not experience the same depression and related problems that have been evident in the past. This plan was discussed with Ernie and he has agreed to this and he has also agreed to remain the hospital for at least another 30 days."

Greg brought this up in team meeting on June 20th because it turned out Vance was on vacation, and Dolph had announced in Monday's meeting that he was leaving to be Director of the Forensic Unit on July 1st, although he was present for this meeting. Everyone on the team agreed with the plan, but Dolph and Greg tried to persuade Dr. Presley that Warren was ready to leave now and if he were to be kept here longer, he would risk going back to the self-destructive institutionalized habits again. Dr. Presley didn't want to hear it because he thought he had to be cautious with Warren.

Dolph then asked, "How about a Conditional discharge of 30 days? We've gotten a lot of people out of here on Conditional discharge and they're still technically hospital patients."

Dr. Presley responded, "If the Morse Center finds out we're doing that, they may not continue him in the program."

Greg stated, "There's got to be some way to ensure he won't self-destruct by keeping him here any longer. He should've been discharged a few months ago."

Dr. Presley countered, "Look, nobody else wants Warren. If it were up to you, you'd try to empty out half of the unit. As long as we have patients, we have jobs."

Dolph and Greg looked at each other and shook their heads, while Cindy and another nurse smiled. Later in the day, however, Dr. Presley told

Greg that depending on how Warren was doing, he might make a deal with the Morse Center next month to release Warren on a 14-day Conditional Discharge, but he would have Vance coordinate such an agreement with them.

Greg saw Warren the next day. He was pleased with his evaluation.

Warren said, "I like the place. Everyone has treated me like a human being there, for a change. But it's time for me to get out of here. I'm a little upset that Dolph is leaving. He gets things done faster. Anyway, this means more money for me. I can't live at the Morse Center right now, but they said they'd help me get a place near there."

"The staff tells me you seem happier and the notes in your chart haven't shown anything negative in a long time. Most of the time they don't see you as much."

"I'm surviving by not being around here as much as possible. Or staying in my room."

"You're not drinking, are you?"

He smiled and said, "I'm going to AA one night a week and every Saturday and Sunday."

"You didn't answer my question."

"You'd be the first one to know if I look like I'm drinking or getting drunk. I'm saving my money for when I get out of here."

A week later he came to Greg's office and started talking about a brother of his who he hadn't seen since he was 12. "Somebody at the Morse Center said they met him. He's over 7 feet tall and weighs 185 pounds."

"Is this you being grandiose again, or was the person who told you joking?"

"I believe it. If I didn't get beaten down so much, maybe I would've been at least a foot taller. This back brace is too tight. That's what stunted my growth. I vomited yesterday because it was too tight. I wear glasses when I'm at work and I see better but the frames are too tight. That's why I have headaches lately."

"I hope the old Warren isn't back from the things you're saying."

"No. I got an appointment with an orthopedic specialist at the M&S building next Tuesday. Like I told you, I want every physical problem I have taken care of before I get out of here."

"How's work going?"

"Real good. A lot of people are going on vacation next week, so I have a chance to look for a place to live there in my spare time next week."

"Don't go AWOL. You'll blow it all. By the way, Vance just came back from vacation, but he's going to be gone away again for a week in July."

"Then I'll make my own discharge plans. I still want to live at the YMCA downtown if I can't get a place near the Morse Center. Even if I have to take a bus back and forth every day to the Morse Center."

"I suggest you talk to Dolph in the next day or two here for any advice about that. His last day is Friday."

"I have an appointment with the mental health clinic near the Morse Center next Tuesday at 9 a.m. Judy got the appointment for me."

"It looks like they really want you to live and work there. Keep yourself under control and be patient."

"My patience is wearing thin lately."

Chapter 19:
AN ETHICAL DILEMMA AND A SURPRISE

On July 5th; it was Greg's day of the week to work 1 to 9 p.m. Not long after he arrived at his office, Warren came by and said, "I have to see you now."

"OK, but you only have about 15 minutes. I have a Medical Records Committee meeting at 1:30."

"I have to speak and tell my story at the AA meeting tonight at 7 o'clock."

"Be honest, not grandiose, when you tell your story."

"I will. Vance told me my Medicaid is running out at the end of the month because I've been here too long. I got to get out of the bughouse – ASAP!"

"I was hoping something like this wouldn't happen."

Warren's voice became louder and more irritated, as he said, "My appointment at the mental health clinic got postponed until next Wednesday at 9 a.m. I was lucky they gave me time off work."

Greg asked, "Isn't Vance looking for a place for you now that Dolph is gone?"

"He's trying to see if David (a former patient) and I can get an apartment together. He says Voc. Rehab. will pay for the security deposit, but they won't give us funds for rent for 3 more weeks. This is pissing me off!"

"Do you want to live with David?"

"Yeah, I'm OK with that, but I don't know if he wants to live with me. We got drunk together one night the last time I was out of here, last year. He almost got arrested and I went to the emergency room of the hospital over there. It's a good thing I'm speaking at AA tonight because I feel like drinking at times. At least work is going good."

"Talk to your sponsor. Do the relaxation exercises, especially just before the meeting. Visualize yourself getting through your talk. About getting out of here, you'll be out soon. Even Dr. Presley is talking about the possibility of discharging you to any living situation as long as you can get to the Morse Center 5 days a week. It's not my role in this system, but if nobody else does anything, I'll see if I can somehow help get you a place to live. In the meantime, do the best job you can at work. Stay away from beer and booze. Try not to get down on yourself – you've done a great job coping with these frustrations so far. Watch out for any grandiose thoughts or verbalizations – don't try to impress or outdo people when you talk. I have to go. Good luck tonight."

As Greg was leaving later that evening, Warren was entering the building and said, "Hey, I just got back from the AA meeting."

"How'd it go?"

"I did good. Later a couple of guys said I was a bullshitter, and that bothered me, but they're ignorant. I told them, "No brag, just facts," and I walked away. My new sponsor said I was fine. A lot of those people don't know what I've been through all these years."

"Hang in there. I'll see you next week."

On the evening of the 12th, at about 8 p.m., Warren came into Greg's office and immediately started bitching and complaining about every little physical problem he experienced over the past decade. Then he got grandiose talking about work, and said how he really should be allowed to run things at the canteen there because he felt he already accomplished, or could achieve, every goal; they set for him through the end of next year. He was standing, gesturing wildly a couple of times, and his voice was rising as he spoke.

Greg asked, "Warren, did you ever hear of Monty Python?"

"Yeah. I snuck out of here a couple of years ago and watched that Holy Grail movie downtown. What's that got to do with anything?"

"That's how you're coming off to me right now – like a Monty Python character. Almost like the first time I met you. I hope you're not doing that with people outside of the hospital, or anywhere."

Warren suddenly calmed down and gave a weak smile.

After a moment, Greg continued, "I'm glad you calmed down the way you did just now. A couple of years ago, you would've stormed out of here. Would you like to share what's really bothering you, other than the fact that you're still stuck here?"

"I've been sick with a cold and sore throat for a couple of days, and I sprained my bad foot again. And don't tell anybody, but I went out and got drunk last night. I went into the Ramada Inn for happy hour and I got a beer. I talked about how I was starting to get a sore throat to the guy next to me at the bar, and he said, 'You know alcohol kills the germs.' So, I switched to two shots of bourbon on the rocks. I knew I had to get out of there and I came in the back door of the building. I'm lucky I didn't fall. I went to bed and slept it off. I didn't go to work today. I refused to take any meds from Joan White because I don't trust her. I took a couple of Bufferins this morning, and I'm not hung over now. I can't miss another day of work or they'll get rid of me."

Greg thought, "What an ethical dilemma."

He said to Warren, "This puts me in a very difficult position. If I tell the staff you went out and got drunk, you won't get out of here, and it'll get back to Vance and the people at the Morse Center. If I say nothing and someone finds out you told me this, I could get a reprimand and my department head might put me on probation. If I leave here and want to come back someday, that will haunt me for any job I try to get in this state system."

"Please don't tell anyone. I'm getting out of here, even if I have to do my own discharge planning."

"What about the shared apartment with David?"

"He doesn't want to do it now. Bob and Steve (a couple of former patients) say they want to live with me. But Bob's living in a tent about a mile or so away from here and he's probably on his way to coming back here. Steve is a loner. He's always more comfortable alone than around any other people, so if we lived together, he'd bolt on me at some point. My other main problem is money. I've got to start saving some."

"So, what did you learn, in terms of going out last night? Was it worth it?"

"No, it wasn't worth it. My sore throat got worse. My foot hurts. I missed work. I won't do it again."

"We have a team meeting tomorrow. Let me sleep on it regarding what, if anything, I'll say when your name comes up for discussion."

"I'm sorry I did it. Please – help me, don't hurt me. I have another interview at the clinic on Monday."

In team meeting, Warren's name did come up about how he had missed work the day before. Greg said, "Keep an eye on him. He's frustrated about still being here and this could be a time when he's vulnerable to start drinking. The longer he stays here, the worse he might feel about himself, and then he'd be prone to slip back into all of the old behaviors. We have to get him out of here before that happens."

Dr. Presley and the off-ward staff agreed, but Cindy and Joan White contended that Warren should stay indefinitely. Greg countered, "If that ever happens, he will fight you until he dies – one way or another."

Dr. Presley declared, "I want to hear from the Morse Center people and Vance (who wasn't present at the meeting) before I make a decision to do anything in terms of discharging him."

That Monday afternoon Warren came back from the Morse Center at 4:15 and limped into Greg's office with a wide smile on his face.

"Wow, looks like you had a good day. How'd it go at the clinic?"

"It was great! They want to start me in the Night Club program for people who've gotten out of the bughouse. But guess what? When I was coming out of the clinic, I saw Midge, and she was coming out of the clinic, too! She was seeing her shrink. She told me she was living near there – alone. Her mother passed away and her father got married again, and she was didn't like his new wife, so she left them a few months ago. She's got a job cleaning at an office building on weekends. We had a cup of coffee together and she wants to get back with me! I got her address – she won't be able to afford a phone until next month. Now I really want to get out of here! I have to talk to Dr. Presley tomorrow!"

"Well, that's great news. In team meeting today I told Vance to tell people at the Morse Center to call Dr. Presley ASAP, and I know Vance was trying to get in touch with them this afternoon. Sounds like you had a great day. That sure was good luck you had running into Midge like that."

"She wants to see me as soon as I get out. I told her it'd be about a week or so. If I had the money I'd go down there and see her this week, but I won't be able to take any time away from the Morse Center when I'm there. She hugged me and kissed me!"

"See Dr. Presley either the first thing in the morning before you go to work, or as soon as you get back tomorrow afternoon. He left for the day. I'll tell him what you told me tomorrow."

"Thanks."

Warren saw Dr. Presley the next morning and told him that he didn't want to wait for Vance to get a place for him with someone else, and also that there would be a room available for him at the YMCA downtown next week. Dr Presley said he not only heard from the Morse Center people who they felt that Warren was doing very well in the program, but also from his new therapist at the clinic who wanted to know when Warren would be discharged. Vance reported to Dr. Presley that he had talked to Don Clark at state Voc. Rehab. about Warren. Mr. Clark told Vance that he could get Warren some "start-up" money in about a week, if Dr. Presley agreed to discharge him. Dr. Presley agreed to give Warren a Conditional Discharge at the end of the month, but related that Warren was free to be on leave from the hospital as soon as he could move into the YMCA unless Vance secured a placement for him at the Moore Center in the interim.

Warren's six month stay at the state hospital, which probably should have lasted only six weeks, appeared to be finally ending.

Chapter 20:
TAKING THINGS INTO HIS OWN HANDS

Late in the afternoon of July 19th, Greg was coming out of the nurses' station after charting some notes. Warren spotted him, as he limped down the hallway and said, "I have to talk to you in your office. Do you have time now?"

"Sure."

As soon as he got inside, he said, "A lot has happened in the past few days. I'm moving into the YMCA downtown next week until Midge and I can get a place together."

"Wow, aren't you moving fast with her? Remember what happened the last time."

"We had two long talks. I hitchhiked down there and back on Saturday and I saw her on my lunch break today. I asked her if we could live together and start all over again. She said 'yes.' I didn't ask her to marry me yet. We agreed we have to see how it goes for a while. I have to see Dr. Presley tomorrow morning before I leave from work to see if he'll put me on Conditional Discharge next week. I have to see him about my meds, anyway."

"Vance has got to make those arrangements. I'll bring it up in team meeting tomorrow."

"No. Vance is only here a day or two a week, and I don't get to see him often enough. I'm moving into the YMCA on the 26th, whether I'm out of here or not. I don't want to have to sign out of here AMA again. I told people at work that I had to take the afternoon off a couple of days ago to have my foot examined here. That appointment got cancelled, so I went downtown to the Social Security office, and I talked to them about getting SSI, food stamps, and my Medicaid renewed. If Dr. Presley approves, Voc. Rehab. will pay for my first 5 weeks at the YMCA, but I hope I won't be there that long."

"I don't believe you did all this. Are you getting grandiose again?"

Hell, no! I started some of this the other day through calls at my therapist's office at the clinic – the guy who wants me in the Night Club program. The rest I did myself. You can call Social Security and State Voc. Rehab. and ask them for yourself. Communication isn't all that good between those places and the hospital. I hope Dr. Presley doesn't get mad that I did all this. All he has to do is say the word, sign the papers, and I'll be gone."

"Ordinarily, everybody would be upset with you, pulling this off – if what you say is true – but almost everybody wants to see you get out of here, except maybe for a couple of nurses. We will definitely discuss this whole situation in team meeting tomorrow."

"Let me write a note to him right now in case, for some reason, I don't get to see him. I know he comes in at 8 o'clock."

Greg handed him a pen and a legal pad. Warren said, "I'm dating this for tomorrow."

He wrote:

"*MEMO*

Dr. Presley:

I know that Social Security, the YMCA, and Don Clark at Voc. Rehab. may have been in touch with you. I am asking you to please put me on Conditional Discharge starting next Thursday, July 26th. Talk to them at the Morse Center, if you want. They'll tell you I'm doing real well and good enough to go. I appreciate all your help with this matter.

But I have two more requests. One is that if you could move my Prolixin shot to every 10 days because I can feel it start to wear off after around 11 or 12 days, and not every 2 weeks. Also, please get me some kind of a grant for $50.00 so I may buy some food at the beginning of August.

Respectfully yours,

Dr. Warren Ernest Irish Le Blanc (signed)

"Warren, you don't start with 'MEMO.' Take that out of there. Any $50 for food would have to go through Vance, or whatever social worker you can convince to get it for you once you're out of here. You say you're going to get food stamps, anyway. Take the 'Dr.' and the 'Irish' out of there on your signature – he'll think you're getting grandiose again."

"I thought the 'MEMO' would get his attention. I need the $50 because food stamps don't start until August 1st. I'm not gonna try to get it gambling. If I ask Midge for $50, she might get rid of me. She doesn't have $50, anyway. I don't know why I put 'Dr.' in there (he laughed)."

"You are so close to leaving here – don't do anything to blow it. I will lobby as hard as I can for Dr. Presley to get you out of here ASAP in the team meeting tomorrow. It's all up to the team tomorrow, and Dr. Presley has the final say."

"I'll slip this note under his door in case I don't get to see him," Warren responded.

"Scratch out the 'MEMO' and 'Dr.' really good so he doesn't know what was there."

In the team meeting the next day, Warren was the first topic of discussion, even though the meeting usually started off with treatment plans for new admissions or anyone scheduled for a treatment plan review. After about 10 minutes of discussion, the vote among people present was 8 to 1 (with only Cindy dissenting) to get Warren out of the hospital on Wednesday. Vance was there, and he said he could get the $50 for Warren next week from hospital funds. Dr. Presley said he would move up Warren's Prolixin shot to 12 days, but it would be the clinic's responsibility for any medication after Warren's discharge. He also said that Warren's Absolute Discharge would be July 31st.

Someone asked, "Vance, did you teach Warren everything you knew about discharge planning?"

Vance started to say that he was busy with so many patients, and Warren was taking up a lot of his time, but Greg countered, "Maybe we should hire Warren as a hospital volunteer in the Social Work department. He'd do a good job. I should ask Larry (Social Work Director)." Everybody laughed.

Warren had the day off from the Morse Center on Wednesday, the 26th, so he could be discharged and move into the YMCA. Greg saw him for his termination session that morning. They went over the chart on his wall about things people need in order to stay out of the state hospital, and by Greg's assessment he had enough to make it independently, at that time. He agreed that he needed to have some help with any of his chronic physical problems, but Morse Center staff could help him, or refer him to a provider who takes Medicaid. He enjoyed his work and training at the Morse Center and he was starting to make friends at AA. He said he had a very supportive AA sponsor.

Greg said, "Hey, I know you probably didn't need to be here this long, but this is the best I've ever seen you, physically and mentally."

"Thanks for your help. I thank Dr. Presley, Dolph, Vance, AA, the Morse Center people, but most of all I'm really glad I got back with Midge. We're good for each other. We're better than we were 3 years ago."

"What do you think you've learned from your stay here this time?"

"I don't ever want to come back here again. I hope the 'revolving door,' as you say, stops now for me. I've seen too many people come in and out of here too many times and some of them even get worse. The biggest thing I learned from you is to think before I act. I can't start drinking. I can't lose my temper – well, I have to control it, at least. Everybody gets mad sometimes. I can't try to one-up people by being 'Mr. Cool.' The first thing I want to do is change my name – I'm going by Ernie now – I told them that at the Morse Center. I want to leave the old 'Warren' behind. Maybe I'll take on Midge's name if we get married. Then I could be 'Midge's Irish' again." He laughed.

"You were out for quite a stretch last time, but you were hanging by a thread a lot of times. Make the decision not to come back, and stick to it. That's how people change their lives, by making serious positive decisions and sticking to them. You wouldn't be the first person to leave this place after being here a long time, never to come back. Use the crisis hot line to call somebody if you need to. If you have five people out there that you can get in touch with at any time – family, friends, AA people, case managers, clinic people – that's a support system."

"By the way, what's this I just heard about you leaving? Now I really don't want to come back here."

"Where'd you hear that? Hardly anyone knows that. I'm gonna tell Dr. Presley today and announce it in team meeting on Friday. I'll still be here until about Labor Day."

"I won't say where I overheard it, but I won't tell anybody. Good luck."

"Good luck to you, too. Hope to run into you again, but not at this place."

They shook hands. Warren moved out an hour later.

In the last part of the team meeting on Monday, July 30th, as they went through the nurses' Kardex (alphabetical order of patients on the ward), Warren's name was announced. Dr. Presley said, "If he doesn't come back by this time tomorrow, I will give him an Absolute Discharge."

Cindy said, "Oh, I hope he stays out, but I bet he'll be back. Maybe he'll be out there longer than the last time, but as soon as he has a fight with his girlfriend or somebody else because of his grandiosity, I bet he'll come limping right through the unit door."

About half of the people in the meeting seemed to agree that they hadn't seen the last of Warren, and they thought he'd be back within a year. Greg said, "I hope it's longer than that – maybe he'll be out forever this time."

One of the ward aides who came to the meeting said, "If it's forever, I hope that means that he won't kill himself someday."

Dr. Presley instructed Greg to do the discharge summary the next morning, since Greg was his primary therapist and treatment plan coordinator. Greg said that he would get it dictated right away and suggested that he and Dr. Presley would "look it over for any corrections, and we'll both sign it."

Dr. Presley stated, "I really hope it's the last time for him. And if he does come back to the hospital again, he'll be in another unit in another building since he's living in a different area of the state now."

Greg spent much of the rest of the day writing the discharge summary. Dr. Presley agreed with everything Greg wrote about a summary of Warren's history, precipitating stress factors for admission, and course in treatment on the unit. However, he disagreed with one of the diagnoses.

"I wouldn't say Depressive Neurosis. He's taking Prolixin IM every 12 days. You have to give him Schizophrenia, Paranoid Type, and add 'in remission.'"

"Yeah, but aside from the occasional grandiosity, he hasn't been psychotic in years."

"That's because the medication is keeping his psychosis in check. Warren even said to me he needed it more often than every two weeks. I could have put him on Navane, but that's a risk of a possible overdose, which he's done before."

"OK, but his primary diagnosis ought to be some kind of mixed personality disorder – DSM-II doesn't have that."

"I hear the new DSM-III next year will have that, but we have to go by DSM-II for now."

"Well, how about 3 different personality disorders: Passive-Aggressive; Explosive; and Inadequate. Also, Episodic Excessive Drinking – not Habitual, and not Alcoholism?"

"OK. We can go with those."

"I left all the physical diagnoses blank. Can you put those in? It's not my area of expertise."

"Yes. I'll take care of that area. His final medication is Prolixin D 25mg. IM q12 days."

Greg put in as recommendations that (a) Warren continue at the Morse Center food service training program until the Morse Center finds him a full- time job. (b) Follow-up with medication, individual psychotherapy, and the "Night Club" program at the mental health clinic. A case manager to meet with him as needed would be helpful. (c) Keep going to AA at least three times a week, and maintain regular contact with his sponsor. (d) Call the local crisis intervention line as needed any hour of the day or night when he feels that he is under a great deal of stress.

Dr. Presley agreed, signed the discharge summary after Greg dictated it, and copies were sent to the mental health clinic and the Morse Center. Greg was much more hopeful about Warren's prospects for staying out of the hospital than he was for any of the other times when Warren was discharged.

Chapter 21:
A NEW BEGINNING AND A NEW NAME

Warren was now "Ernie" – W. Ernest Le Blanc. The state hospital patient was "Warren" and he swore he would never go back there again. Soon after he left the hospital grounds, he resided at the YMCA downtown in the same room where he had lived several years earlier. Even though he was discharged from the hospital, the Morse Center arranged for him to be transported temporarily to and from the YMCA every Monday through Friday, even working around his clinic appointments and AA meetings. He spent every Saturday and Sunday with Midge, staying at her little apartment while she went to work and he took the last bus available back to the YMCA Sunday night. Ernie was so busy, and so tired at night, that he didn't have time to drink, or go out and play pool, or gamble, or hang out anywhere. Except for a few brief verbal skirmishes which were quickly nipped in the bud by staff at the Morse Center, he was doing great at his job. He kept all his appointments and hungered for times he could spend with Midge. She couldn't wait to see him every Saturday. They were falling in love again.

Near the end of August, there was still no vacancy for him to reside at the Morse Center, and they were not willing to provide transportation for him after Labor Day weekend. He decided to meet with staff there and told them that he was planning to move in with Midge, who was about to rent another small apartment about three blocks away from the Morse Center. When he told them that he was ready to move in with her on Labor Day, one staff member worried that he might be rushing things and that he would be set up to fail. However, his supervisor acknowledged that this had been Ernie's plan for the past 6 weeks, and that he was doing so well that the Morse Center staff should support his plans.

Ernie was elated when he got the "go ahead" to proceed with his plan. He kept telling himself, "Don't blow it this time. You've got a good thing going. You like the Morse Center, the staff, the people you're work-ing with, and you have support from Midge, Judy (his supervisor), Jerry (his therapist at the clinic), George (his AA sponsor), Danny (coordina-tor of the Night Club program), and you're starting to make a couple of new friends at the canteen. The hospital and all those people are gone, for you. Don't forget about all the help you got from Greg, Dolph, Jack, Vance and Gina, though. People want you to make it." On the morning of Labor Day, he persuaded George to help move Midge's clothes and furniture to her new apartment. George also helped Ernie and his two loaded, battered suitcases to move out of the YMCA. Once they were in the new apartment, they hugged and kissed. He said, "I'm Ernie forever now. I want to be a regular guy, living a regular life, with a regular lady."

Midge responded, "And I'm an average woman with a good guy for a boyfriend. We're starting off a lot better than we did last time."

That fall was the happiest time period ever for them. Midge did most of the cleaning; Ernie did most of the cooking. Midge's therapist at the clinic saw them together a few times when there were "flare-up" issues that many couples have – money, sex, disagreeing on what to do with their time, friends, etc. Each issue seemed to be resolved in only a session or two. Ernie's therapist, Jerry, emphasized personal growth and ways Ernie could improve his life. They had an outreach case manager who checked to see how they were functioning in the community every couple of weeks. The Night Club had some fun activities, a support group, and some cooperative group projects. Ernie liked his AA group, and George met with him for coffee and breakfast at a local McDonald's every week. Ernie and Midge started to make a few acquaintances who even dropped by their place a few times. They didn't have much money, but they both felt "normal." Ernie saved up to buy Midge a 13-inch color TV for Christmas. She got him a second-hand bicycle with a lock, even though he couldn't ride it much in the winter. They were like a late 20th century Bob Cratchit family without the kids, and to them, it was wonderful.

The next year started off a little rocky. Midge liked her job, but not the hours and having to work weekends. She wasn't making any friends in her age group – all her work associates and people she met at the clinic were about 15 to 20 years or more older than her. Ernie started to vocalize more often that he could run the whole canteen alone, or that he could probably supervise others. He had to be reminded about the terms of the plan the Morse Center had for him, and that even though his probation period had passed, any significant increase regarding responsibilities and independence at work would not be granted until the end of the year. Ernie kept track of the finances they had, although they did not have a joint checking account. Neither one could be issued a credit card due to their spotty, or lack of, full-time work history. They decided that they had to get 40 hour a week jobs (if they could tolerate that) and keep them for a year, but Midge would have a better chance at landing such a position than Ernie.

Midge talked Ernie out of leaving the Morse Center late in March – at one point he said, during an argument with her, "What are they gonna do, send me back to the bughouse? There's no grounds for that!"

"Please don't ruin what we have. The past year has been the happiest I've been in a long time – maybe my whole life!"

"I feel like I'm getting stuck in a rut at the Morse Center. I know as much about running the canteen as anyone in that place does. I'm not gonna do this for years."

"It hasn't even been a year yet. Talk to Judy. Talk to Jerry. Every job has its ups and downs periods. You of all people should know that. I want to move on because we need more money and I want more normal daytime working hours, like most people. We don't see enough of each other, except for during the day on Saturday and Sunday and a couple hours in the evening a few days during the week."

"I should be bringing in more money than you. The man's supposed to do that."

"Not anymore. That's old. You admitted that last year."

"Maybe I can get a part-time job on Saturday nights."

"We can't both be gone Saturday nights. Remember a couple of months ago when somebody tried to break in and you scared them away?"

"Maybe we can get a dog."

"No, we can't do that. We can't afford a dog, vet bills, another mouth to feed, and a dog ties you down for 10 years. I grew up with a dog. It's hard. It causes a lot of fighting."

"This is frustrating. There are times I feel like just cutting loose and getting drunk."

"Please don't ever try to do that. If you end up back in the state hospital, you'll ruin everything we worked so hard for! We can get through this rough time. If you feel like drinking, call George."

Ernie resignedly said, "You're right. It's better than the bughouse. I'm tired of being tired and bored lately. I see Jerry in a couple of days."

"One good thing - none of your physical problems are acting up since you left the hospital."

"I got the usual aches and pains I've had, especially during the winter. I haven't complained to you about them yet. It's a good thing this winter has been a mild one."

"We got to keep helping each other out. I love you, Ernie."

"I love you, too, Midge."

Midge went out to look for a better paying daytime job a few days later. Ads in the local paper didn't help because she didn't drive. Her search was limited to the downtown area (the population of the city where she and Ernie were now living was about 90,000 people). The state employment office was more helpful, but the counselor told her that given her spotty work history, she would be better off staying at her present job for several more months. She told Midge that if she had worked in her present job for a year or more, and if she were to get a good recommendation from her supervisor plus another reference from someone at the clinic, she would have a better chance of landing a more desirable job. Midge was a little disappointed at this assessment, but understood the counselor's reasoning. Ernie, upon hearing this, told Midge that all state agencies are probably prejudiced against anyone who's been in and out of the "bughouse," and that she'd be better off cold calling businesses or trying to start her own business, since they now had a phone. Midge decided not to look for work until the end of the summer. This issue created some tension and arguments a few times during the rest of the year, usually arising when Ernie had a stressful day at the Morse Center.

That Christmastime was rewarding for the both of them. Midge got a full-time job working days as a housekeeper at a large hotel within several blocks of their residence. She had varying days off each week, but she had benefits – health care, sick time, and two weeks' vacation. Ernie, with encouragement from Midge, some Morse Center people, his AA sponsor, and his therapist at the clinic, finally got his GED. He left the Morse Center right after his 18-month contract expired, and with good references from them, started working at a small restaurant downtown. It was open only for breakfast and lunch – 6:00 a.m. to 2:30 p.m. The place had only five employees; no more than four people worked there on any given day, and they were closed Sundays. Unfortunately, he had no benefits except for 10 days of vacation time and holidays off. He had a rotating day off every week, but he would be on call for overtime if someone called in sick. 1981 looked promising for them.

In Ernie's mind, the "bughouse" and everyone affiliated with it (except for Midge and a couple of former patients) were in his rear-view mirror and fading fast. His main source of support was from George, a "big brother" type only a few years older than him. He still saw the same therapist at the clinic, but sessions were now every few weeks because Jerry was promoted to an administrative position. He and Midge both went to the regular Night Club sessions the clinic offered, and in the support group part of the program, they offered helpful hints to some other former state hospital people about adjusting to living back in the community again. Occasionally either he, Midge, or both would miss a session due to mild illnesses or injuries, but their case manager would check on them to see if they were doing OK. Both called the crisis line a couple of times in 1981. Ernie called after a couple of hostile shouting encounters with a customer once, and another time when he was blaming himself for not always being able to fulfill Midge's sexual desires – to his own standards. The beatings he took from staff and patients years ago affected his sexual functioning somewhat. Midge called at one point because she was losing sleep over not having the courage to ask her supervisor for a raise, and later in the year one night crying over the fact that she hadn't made a "best friend" of all the ladies at work or in the clinic. For the most part, however, they had a good year and were happy with the lives they were living.

It was a rough winter in New England and although there weren't many below zero nights, it seemed the snowstorms kept on coming - right until early April. Several times Ernie and Midge missed work because of this. If they didn't work, or if Ernie's restaurant was closed, they didn't get paid. This also cut into any vacation time they were to set aside for the summer. Because money was tight, they had to keep the thermostat lower than in the past two winters. Fortunately, they could buy warm clothes and blankets through the Salvation Army store. Several times Ernie was tempted to buy some whiskey or bourbon to help stay warm (so he said), but after a few arguments, Midge talked him out of it.

In the spring, just as they started eating at different church suppers or breakfasts twice a week because they were trying to stretch money as much as they could, Ernie was promoted to Assistant Manager of the restaurant. He not only got a raise in salary, along with any tips from customers when he served them, but he also had more responsibilities. He had to be at the restaurant every morning a half hour before it opened, inventory all the supplies, receive goods from distributors, check the cleanliness of the premises, brew the coffee, and make sure that everything was in operating order before turning on the lights and opening the door at 6:00 a.m. All the employees, except for one part-timer who worked 3 days a week from 10 a.m. to 2 p.m. (a friendly lady who Ernie now supervised) came in several minutes before the days' opening. It was stressful for him at first, and there were times when his veneer of bravado had to be quelled by his boss, but by the end of the summer it was pleasantly routine. Fortunately, all the employees seemed to get along with each other.

However, things were not going quite as well for Midge. She started feeling depressed because she was dealing with a new supervisor who was a former co-worker. Midge didn't particularly care for her occasional openly negative criticisms of other employees, guests, hotel management, and working conditions. The job became a real "job." There was turnover in her department every few months. She was not the recipient of much open hostility, except for occasional remarks that she wasn't making up the rooms fast enough. By nature, she was the opposite of Ernie when it came to dealing with people – she learned to do her job, shut her mouth, and hope for the best regarding tips guests left. She had no co-workers with whom she could commiserate, and few reached out to her to engage in typical social pleasantries. Ernie, the people at the Night Club at the clinic, and her therapist were the only people she trusted, and she and Ernie started having some arguments when they came home from work. One night in September she called the crisis line and she wondered if she should go back to the state hospital voluntarily after the call ended.

Ernie pleaded with her, "Midge, don't do it. We had an agreement that neither one of us can go back to the bughouse. If you go, you might not get out for a long time – who knows? Your boss might fire from you. There won't be any health benefits if that happens. Look, we both have about four days left to use of vacation time until the end of the year. You can take time off."

"I don't know how much longer I can take it," she cried.

"Not every day has been a bad day there or you would've quit months ago. If you need to look for another job, use the time off you got coming to you. Do you want me to go over there and complain? I'll raise hell with your boss and the hotel manager! Do you want to see if we can hire you? I'll supervise you."

"No, you can't go over to the hotel. They'll think you're some kind of nut and get you arrested and send you back to the hospital again. I either have to work at another hotel so I can get tips or get a better paying job. And I can't be a waitress at your place – that's too much stress for me. What happens if we start arguing in front of customers? I don't want to work at any kind of eating place – not even a McDonald's."

"Don't take any crap from your supervisor – go higher up on her and bitch about a lot of people quitting lately."

"I don't want to be a troublemaker. I'll take Friday off and look. I'll take a bus to the mall and see if any places there are hiring. I've gotta do something."

Ernie hugged her and said, "We're gonna get through this. We have to. The two of us on my salary won't be enough to survive, especially with colder weather coming. I hope the landlord doesn't raise the rent.

I don't wanna go back to doing any side hustles like I did when I was in the bughouse."

Chapter 22:
ARE THINGS STARTING TO GO DOWNHILL?

The late summer of '82 produced more changes. Midge got another job in the housekeeping department at another hotel, but she had to work two weekends every month. This left her time off together with Ernie only one full weekend a month and one day a month during the week when they both happened to have a Thursday off. Midge had the same salary and benefits as her last job, but her tips brought in more money because the hotel was more "upscale" than her last place of employment. She fortunately was able to procure rides to and from work with a couple of older friendly co-workers. Only rarely did she have to take a bus with a long walk to and from work.

Ernie started becoming bored with his job. He became grouchy once in a while with co-workers and even a few times with customers. His manager, Matt, who owned the little restaurant, had to pull Ernie aside twice for the sarcastic or rude remarks he made.

Matt, one day after closing time, said, "Ernie, you're good at your job, but you're getting irritable more lately. Whenever you're around customers, watch your mouth. I feel the same way you do about things that piss you off, but if you start driving people away from here, I might have to let you go."

Ernie responded, "Some of these people complain about the food not being the way they like, or the service being slow, but the hell with them. We don't need their business. Carrie, that girl you hired last month, just doesn't have it. She doesn't learn as fast as she should. It's frustrating when I have to work with her when we're busy – 7:30 to 9, and 11:30 to 1o'clock."

"Do not make any snide remarks about her in front of the customers. It's bad for business. Don't go telling people if they don't like what they ordered that they can go to McDonald's. One of the first things you learn is that the customer's always right - even if they aren't."

"We have more people coming in here that are a pain in the ass than there used to be."

"Business is better than it used to be, so you have more good customers, and more that are a pain in the ass. Maybe you shouldn't work the counter as much – just be on the grill more and do other things in the back room."

"No, please don't do that. It'll take away from the tips I get."

"I'm just saying you're good, and I'll have your back, but you ought to clean up your act a little."

Things got better for Ernie after that talk, and some sessions with Jerry helped. He also admitted to Jerry that he had self-esteem issues flaring up because Midge was making more money than him lately. At least he managed the finances for the couple and did a good job, according to Elaine, their case manager. Elaine was a nurse in an outreach role at the clinic.

However, in November, Jerry announced he was leaving the clinic for a job in Portland. At Thanksgiving, George "fell off the wagon." This "double whammy" hit Ernie hard. He lobbied to see if he could get Danny to be his therapist, but his caseload was full. A new young psychologist named Ralph was to add Ernie to his caseload, but as a throwback to his old attitudes, Ernie seemed cynical and implied that he knew more than Ralph did about mental health. Ralph, being right out of school, was slightly arrogant (as many young relatively inexperienced psychologists are), and the first few sessions did not go smoothly. Ernie started going to happy hours at the Ramada Inn, and having a drink with his food, against Midge's arguing and threatening to walk home alone. On one of his days off in December, he bought a six pack of beer and hid it outside in a pile of snow in back of their apartment near the garbage can. He started missing AA meetings and instead dropped into a downtown bar to have a beer. He grudgingly went to the Night Club meetings with Midge and expressed some resentment toward Danny because he wouldn't be his therapist. Matt noticed that Ernie was "going through the motions" at work, not being as communicative with employees and customers as he usually was. Ernie admitted to him that except for most days at work, things were not going well lately, and he said, "Right now I can function better if I mostly do my job, shut my mouth, and go home." Ernie didn't want to talk with Matt about the situations in his life. Matt knew Midge and felt uncomfortable calling her, but he knew that Ernie had a case manager from the clinic, and he encouraged him to talk to her, or else call the crisis line at night if needed.

A week before Christmas, Elaine, of all people, discovered several cans of Ernie's six pack in a melting snowbank when she went to throw out a bag of fast food remains into their garbage can after she parked her car outside their residence. She confronted Ernie, who lied about the beer at first, but then Midge started crying and begged Ernie to say if this were true. An argument started, but after several minutes Ernie admitted that he had started drinking because he lost Jerry and George and felt rejected by Danny. One of his friends who used to be a patient at the state hospital saw him coming out of a bar a few nights before, and he told Midge, but Ernie denied this when she confronted him. It was a longer than usual session with Elaine. Midge said she would leave Ernie "if you ever pulled this crap again." Ernie was remorseful and agreed he would quit drinking. He couldn't afford to leave his job to go into a 28-day substance abuse program. He swore that he wasn't getting drunk or hung over, or missing work. He agreed to go back to AA and get another sponsor. He agreed to call the crisis line in the evening or on his days off if things were bothering him. He would go to the clinic and ask for a new therapist. Elaine would see them once a week and call them once a week.

It was not a good winter for Ernie. After an angry session with Ralph, and lingering anger over Danny's refusing to be his therapist, he decided to have no more involvement with the clinic except for Elaine. In February, with Elaine's negotiations and Midge's pleading, he agreed to see a new therapist at the clinic, Arnie. Ernie did not want to go back to the Night Club, however. A long time AA member, Rick, agreed to take Ernie on as his sponsor, but he said it would be a few weeks because he had to travel to Illinois. Before Rick left, he urged Ernie to go to every AA meeting he could until he returned, given Ernie's recent slip-up. Ernie was uncomfortable with the younger people in the group, and one night he almost got in a fight with two other guys – one of them confronted him about his time in the state hospital and the other man teased him about being "crazy," and "a liar." An older member broke up the altercation and drove Ernie home, even though it was only four blocks away. Ernie went to a late afternoon group that met at a church near his job three times a week until Rick got back. Fortunately, Ernie stayed dry through mid-March. He sat next to Rick every meeting and both of the guys who were bothering him dropped out of AA.

Ernie's job got to be monotonous. His only enjoyable time at work consisted of short-order cooking and talking with several regular customers. Most of the time, when he came home from work, he felt tired and achy, but he was convinced he could get a better job either as a manager or working at a better restaurant. Many times, when Midge came home from work, he would start griping about his job and going on and on about how one of these days he would quit. Midge would argue with him for a brief period, then go into their bedroom sobbing for about an hour before things calmed down.

Midge liked her job and the people with whom she was working. At times, she seemed happier at work than at home. She still went to the Night Club and still had the same therapist, who occasionally suggested that Ernie should come into the sessions to discuss conflicts between Midge and him, but Ernie refused. He said that he was exhausted from his job, his aches and pains, AA meetings and bi-monthly sessions with Arnie (who he liked, because Arnie once worked at a state hospital in Connecticut and "he understands me"). Elaine still saw them once a month and questioned Ernie about whether his relationship with Midge was still a priority in his life.

"Yeah, but stress of all this crap is grinding me down. I'm tired. I'm hurtin.' Not much is fun anymore. Sometimes I feel like I'm living out the string of days, but I don't want to be like that."

"You didn't really answer the question. Do you love Midge?"

"Yes. She's keeping me out of the bughouse."

Midge cried, "Is that all of what I am to you now? Keeping you out of the hospital?"

"No, no, I love you. You know that. Life is hard for me right now."

"That's the first time you said, 'I love you' to me since Christmas."

"I'll always be Midge's Irish, no matter what." Ernie moved over to the couch and hugged Midge.

Midge smiled, kissed him, and said to Ernie that she loved him. Elaine strongly suggested that they see either Arnie or Jane (Midge's therapist at the clinic) for sessions as a couple. She commended them on not falling into financial trouble, in spite of their meager salaries, and that their living conditions appeared to be clean and not in disrepair. Elaine also said that Midge's health seemed good, and both of them were complying with their medications, but she recommended that Ernie see a physician at a local new walk-in clinic not far away ("They take Medicaid there.").

Over the next few months, things went better for Ernie and Midge, as Ernie followed Elaine's suggestions. Ernie's feelings about his job did not improve, however. More often than not, he still felt emotionally exhausted from a day's work. Except for most of the regular customers, he was not always polite or welcoming. He felt that for all the work he was doing for Matt, he could have been given more support or recognition. He wondered if Matt felt that he was a "pain in the ass" at times, instead of the eager employee he hired a few years ago.

Then, one day in July, Matt said he was retiring and selling the place at the end of the month to Kenny, an acquaintance who had owned a similar restaurant in another town in the state. Kenny and Ernie clashed right away - about changes in the menu, how to cook certain breakfast meals, fraternizing with regular customers, supervising a couple people out of high school working for the summer, and even about taking inventory. After the first week in August, Ernie started loudly complaining to Midge that he couldn't stand working for Kenny much longer. Midge thought if he really felt that way, maybe he should look for another job on his day off. Only one of the other part-time employees felt the same way about Kenny as Ernie, though, so Ernie couldn't lead a revolt at work. Arguing with Kenny brought back memories of his clashes with some of the nurses in the state hospital. Work was getting to be an unhappy place.

At 11 o'clock on August 15th, Ernie started walking out of the restaurant.

Kenny asked, "Where the hell are you going?"

"I'm on break. I've been here over 5 hours and by law you owe me break time. Besides, I'm Catholic, this is a Holy Day of Obligation, and I'm going to church. By law, you can't deny me that time off."

Before Kenny could respond, Ernie went out to the back of the restaurant, got on his bike, and rode away. He didn't go to church. He went to a bar not far away from his house. After several beers, he started getting drunk, and he became loud and argumentative with some people at the bar, as well as the bartender – mainly about how to run the bar's kitchen. When one guy at the bar threatened to fight him, the bartender threw Ernie out. When he got outside, he was shocked to see that his bicycle was gone. Ernie let out a loud, cursing scream, as he saw what was left of a broken chain on the side of a fence in the alley next to the bar. Somebody came out of the bar and yelled to Ernie that he better go home before the cops came. Ernie hobbled home crying and he went to bed immediately.

After Midge came home from work, she aroused Ernie from his nap.

"What are you doing in bed?"

"I'm sick. I don't want to talk about it."

"Was it something at work that happened?"

"I said I don't want to talk about it!"

"Who's making dinner tonight, you or me?"

"I don't want to eat. Get something for yourself. Leave me alone and let me sleep!"

A couple of hours later, Midge took the garbage out, and she noticed Ernie's bike wasn't there. She went in the bedroom and cried out, "Ernie, where's your bike?"

Ernie groggily responded, "Somebody stole it."

She excitedly asked, "What? From here or from work?"

"It's gone," he said, as he started to get out of bed, bleary-eyed.

"Tell me what happened! Something happened to you today."

"You don't want to hear it."

"I do! And don't lie to me! Did you have a real bad day at work with Kenny?"

"I don't work there anymore."

Midge cried, "What do you mean you don't work there anymore?"

Ernie then told her the whole story of what transpired earlier. Midge was very upset, crying loudly, saying to him that in one day Ernie was destroying their whole world. She said she warned Ernie months ago that if he ever started drinking again that they'd have to split up because she couldn't take anything that would destroy their relationship. She told him he better go to an AA meeting that night, but he said it was too late. He promised he would call Rick. Midge said that if he didn't call the crisis line tonight, she would call for herself. She urged him to get in touch with Kenny tonight or show up tomorrow morning and talk to him about resolving their issues. He said that he wasn't going back there and he wouldn't even call him because Kenny would fire him on the spot. Midge told him that if he didn't get another job by the end of the month, they would be through as a couple and one of them would have to move out of the apartment. Ernie had an appointment with Arnie later in the week. Midge said she would call Jane ASAP or maybe Elaine. She emphasized, "You need help now! And I need help! How could you do this to yourself and us?"

"I'm not talking about today anymore. I just want to stay in bed and sleep. I feel like crap. I'm sorry. I'll look for a job and deal with life tomorrow."

REBOUNDING

Ernie got out of bed at 5:30 and started to plot his strategy for what he should do to reassemble the shattered pieces of his life. He thought, "I really screwed up this time. I have a place to live, I have Midge if she doesn't get rid of me soon, and nothing else. I know Elaine is gonna be almost as pissed at me as Midge is. Arnie, too, probably. I gotta call Rick. He told me he had a relapse before. Then I got to go to the library and look in the want ads in the paper. If I don't get a job right after Labor Day, there might not be enough money to pay all the bills with just Midge's salary."

Before she went to work, Midge pleaded with him to call Rick and call Arnie. She said, over Ernie's objections, that she would get in touch with Elaine to see if she could come over to see them tomorrow afternoon. Ernie called Rick and met him at the McDonald's not far away for a cup of coffee. After Ernie told him his tale of woe, Rick said something to the effect that slip-ups happen to most people in AA, but "be sure this is the only one if you want to successfully quit for good." He further said that in a way this was not unlike people you saw in the state hospital who came back there because they stopped taking their medication. He encouraged him to call Arnie because, "You're lucky somebody didn't call the cops and send you to jail or back to the state hospital. I'm glad you got in touch with me." Ernie nodded his head a few times dismissively and told him sadly, "I lost my bike, I lost my job, and I might be losing Midge. I need a job. I need money." Rick told him to come to the meeting tonight at the Methodist church, and that he'd ask around for him about anyone who might be able to hire him soon, "but call Arnie."

Ernie walked off what was left of his hangover and limped into the library. He looked in the want ads of today's newspaper as well as the Sunday paper. "Nothing," he thought. Then he went to the branch of the State unemployment office. He stood in line for 15 minutes before he got frustrated and asked someone to help him use one of the microfilm machines where available jobs were listed. The only restaurant job was at a Burger King at the food court in the mall, but he'd have to take a bus back and forth to get there. That gave him the idea to go to the mall tomorrow and look for other sales jobs there ("I can sell," he thought), but he would have to call Matt to ask him for a reference. He hobbled home and called Matt, who was still in the area. Matt wasn't in but luckily, he had an answering machine, so Ernie left a message for Matt to call him ASAP. He stayed home and waited for Matt to call. He felt too embarrassed to call Arnie, and he was seeing him at the clinic in a few days, anyway. Midge came home, and after a brief argument, Ernie said that he saw Rick and was going to the AA meeting tonight – Rick would pick him up outside the house and drive him home later.

At the meeting, Ernie didn't get up and speak, but he and Rick asked around to see if they knew of anyone who might be hiring. One guy told him to try the Subway downtown. They had a college kid working there who was about to leave to go back to school out of town. Nobody else knew of any openings. When Ernie got home, Midge said Matt called and that he would give him a recommendation, but "he said to tell you never quit a job again unless you have another one to go to." Matt told Midge that he didn't know of anyone who was hiring, and that Kenny would probably never take him back.

"I'm going to the mall tomorrow. I don't want to work at Subway unless there's nothing else anywhere," Ernie said to Midge.

"Beggars can't be choosers. You got to get a job!" she replied.

The next day, Ernie put on his best clothes and took a bus to the mall, arriving at 10:30. It seemed to be perfect timing because most stores had relatively few customers at that time of the day. After getting shot down at 5 places, he ate a pretzel at the food court and limped into a shoe store. The store was almost empty with only the cashier, one salesman and the manager on the floor. Ernie was very polite when he asked the manager if he needed any help, and although he did not have experience selling shoes, he did have about three years of experience as assistant manager of a small restaurant downtown. When Ernie named the place where he worked, the manager, smiled and said, "You look familiar. A lot of mornings I used to stop in there on my way to the store to get a coffee and English muffin to go and maybe you're the guy who waited on me most of the time. Do you know Matt?"

"Matt was my boss. He was our manager until he sold the place a couple of months ago."

"Yeah. I was just checking to see if you weren't b.s.ing me. I know Matt. Now I remember you. I thought you gave good customer service. How come you're not there today?"

"I left there last week. It wasn't the same without Matt and the new owner had different ways of doing things. I wasn't the only one who quit."

He shook Ernie's hand and said, "My name's Craig," and he pulled out an application for employment out of a drawer below the Cashier's desk. Craig gave him a clipboard and told him to fill out the application, saying, "I don't have anything open full-time, but I have a couple of college kids who're working here and they're are going away to school in two weeks, so if I can talk to Matt first, there's a possibility I might hire you part-time and train you. It won't be until after Labor Day, though. No guarantees on working here, yet. Go ahead and fill this out over there, and bring it back to me."

Ernie filled out the application, putting his work experience down as only at the Morse Center and the restaurant. For education, he wrote in that he had a GED. When Craig looked at the application, he said, "Whoa – what'd you do before you were 29?"

"Well, I quit school when I was a teenager and just had some odd jobs once in a while – no more than a couple of weeks at a time here and there, and after I got my GED, I went to the Morse Center because I decided it was time I finally got trained for a steady job."

"I have to call Matt."

"Good. I'm sure he'll give me a good reference. How soon can you get back to me?"

"I got your phone number"

"Thanks, Craig."

Ernie couldn't bring himself to go to the Burger King at the Mall, so he went outside, waited for the next bus to bring him back to downtown, and went home. Later that afternoon, he started looking in the phone book and writing down any places that might hire him as a short order cook or as a clerk in a store. He was excited about the possibility of working in a shoe store, even though he would have to take a bus to get back and forth to the mall, but he knew he needed a full-time job. "Maybe I can get two part-time jobs," he thought.

Elaine came by late the next afternoon, and was visibly upset at Ernie when he and Midge told her about the events of Monday.

She subtly berated him for the poor judgment he used and how he didn't consider the burden the outcome of the events put on Midge. "You don't realize how close you could have come to getting sent back to the state hospital or doing time in jail if the cops showed up at that bar," she said.

"You don't have to harp on me. What's done is done. I don't need a two against one on me here. Besides, I'm looking for another job."

Midge added, "Ernie, I know you – if you're out of work or not doing something with your life, it'd be so easy for you to start drinking and gambling again, and where does that leave us?"

Ernie responded loudly, "Give me a chance to get back on my feet! I'm trying!"

Elaine talked about the possibility of getting SSI Disability again or Welfare ("You won't be able to get unemployment because you quit your job."), and she urged him to show up for his appointment with Arnie tomorrow, as well as AA meetings.

Arnie saw him the next afternoon and he took the approach, "What happens now? I want you to tell me the consequences of your behavior, and what you learned from this."

Ernie agreed that the episode of anger on Monday and the relapse of alcohol abuse "were damn dumb things to do. My own AA sponsor said most people relapse at least once. That's no excuse, though. I'm looking for work so that I can help pay the bills, get another bike, don't do anything to hurt Midge so badly again, and try to live a normal life."

"You may have heard something like this in AA before, but don't drink - think!"

"Yeah. Next time I'm in that situation, I'll call the crisis line, or Rick, or somebody for help."

"It's all a matter of being in control – not out of control. Does alcohol put you in control?"

"After a couple of beers or drinks it helps temporarily, but then I want more and I do crazy things."

"What about before that? What could you have done differently when you were angry at Kenny?"

"It started a few weeks or so before that. I should've looked for another job all those afternoons I just went home and stewed with my anger. Maybe there would've been some other job open then."

"I think you and Midge should keep seeing Elaine as a couple. In the meantime, I want to see you same time next week, OK? We'll take it week to week for a while. If you need help, call the crisis line, or call Rick if you feel the urge to drink. It's good that you like AA and have a sponsor who cares."

"All right. I got the message. I need all the help I can get."

Ernie kept looking for work for the rest of the week, and came up empty. Midge kept telling him to "get something, anything. Even if it's at one of the fast-food places to hold you over until you get something else. We can't make it on just my salary. We won't be able to pay the rent through the end of the year." Ernie kept telling her to be patient. He promised her that he would try the burger joints if he came up empty at the end of the week.

In Friday night's AA meeting, Ernie got up and told the story of his recent relapse. When the meeting was over, a man came to him and said, "I like the way you told your story. You sound more convincing than some of these other people who give the impression, 'I slipped up, ha ha.' Now you say you're out of work, and I might be able to help. My name's Keith. I'm the program director for radio 1350 downtown. Do you listen to our DJs?"

"Yeah, sometimes when I have the radio on. I don't have an FM radio, though."

"We're an AM station. Right now, I think we could use somebody to help out on Sundays."

"You want me to be a DJ? Wow! I never did anything like that before."

"No, no – you'd have to have training, and an FCC license for that. I'm talking about a 'gofer' person – get coffee, sodas, snacks, sandwiches and supplies for the DJs – Dick and Cindy – and do a lot of other little things, like help organize their schedule for that day, answer the phone and take messages – especially for any news, weather and sports updates to pass along, and maybe even help get them records or the new CDs to play. Do some cleaning, too. You'd be busy, with some breaks. You think you'd be interested?"

"Yeah, but I'd need more than a minimum wage salary."

"Well, I might be able to get you around $8.00 an hour, 8 a.m. to 4:30 p.m., but I have to talk to John, our station manager, first. Come to the meeting Monday night, and I'll let you know what he says."

"Sure, I'll be here," Ernie said, excitedly.

Midge thought it was good news that Ernie had some leads on jobs, but she told him that "doesn't mean they'll hire you." Ernie responded that he would still keep looking, but if he came up empty, and the other part-time jobs came through for him, "all I'd need is one other minimum wage job one day a week, and for four days a week, I'll be making more than I did at the restaurant." She thought it was a bad idea to have three part-time jobs, with two days idle when she wouldn't be around, but he thought he could pull it off with no problems, if it came to that.

Keith was at the AA meeting Monday night. He motioned Ernie to get in his car afterwards.

"If you're still interested, John wants to meet you. Come by the station Friday morning at about 10. Here's an application for employment – fill it out and bring it in with you."

"Thanks, Keith. I know where it is. I'll be there. I want to work there, even if it's only a day a week."

"I can't promise you anything, but we really need someone to do miscellaneous stuff and I put in a good word for you. I don't know if he's looking to interview anyone else, but it's hard to get somebody to work Sundays."

"I'll be there. I'll wear a sport coat and tie."

"You don't have to do that – just casual dress, but clean and presentable. He's a pretty laid-back guy. Good luck."

He told Midge, "If they hire me, that's a start."

Midge said, "Yeah, but one day a week doesn't cut it for us."

"I'm going back to the unemployment office tomorrow to see if anything else has turned up."

He secured two leads. The first place, a diner, was about a 7 block walk away from his house, but the manager said he had just hired someone. He went into a little coffee shop down the street that had a "Help Wanted" sign in the window. Ernie asked to see the manager about the opening, and introduced himself to the guy.

Immediately, the man said, "I heard about you. Kenny told me you went out on a break and never came back, and he heard you went out and got drunk at some bar. That doesn't do wonders for your reputation, pal. You think I'd actually hire you? You got balls coming in here."

Ernie shot back, "Who the hell are you, his brother?" He stormed out the door, wondering if anyone would hire him at any of the downtown food establishments.

The next day he thought that maybe he could apply for work as a janitor, if worst came to worst. He was getting anxious and worried. He had to get some kind of minimum wage job, full-time or part-time that he could physically perform. On Thursday morning, as Ernie was about to pound the pavement again, Craig called.

"Hey, Ernie, I talked to Matt. He convinced me to take a chance on you part-time. Another part-timer I have is leaving after Labor Day, so I could train you, but you'd be working here Wednesdays and Saturdays - 16 hours a week. How's that sound to you?"

"That's great, Craig. When do I start?"

"September 7th. C'mon in right when the store opens at 10. You won't be on the floor selling shoes for the first two weeks, but I'll have you get familiar with our stock, and have you shifting shoe boxes, and learning other things. The Wednesday after Labor Day is always slower than usual, but Saturday is always a busy day. You'll be working 10 to 5:30 both days."

"This is more than minimum wage, I hope, isn't it?"

"$3.35 an hour and 8% of everything you sell beyond $1000 worth of shoes, polish, or handbags per week. If you work out OK selling, you might be making good part-time money when business really picks up in the fall right through Christmas."

"I will be there on September 7th. Thanks a lot, Craig."

Ernie didn't bother to look for work that day. It was comforting that he had at least one new work situation. Maybe the radio station would come through for him, too. He eagerly showed up at the AM station right on time the next morning. After he introduced himself to the receptionist, Carla, she said with a smile they were expecting him. She buzzed Keith, who came right out to meet him.

"Ernie, you look good, Let's go see John," Keith said, as he shook his hand with a grin.

Down the hall and around the corner was John's office, smaller than Ernie expected, but with autographed pictures of various pop music stars on the wall and a copy of Billboard magazine on his desk. He was just hanging up the phone when Keith introduced Ernie to him. John was a big guy, about 40, with a wide smile and a firm handshake. He wanted to know about Ernie personally, how long he lived in the area, and If Ernie listened to their station.

"Sure. I have an AM radio at home, not an FM. I like Elton John. 'I'm Still Standing' is my favorite song this year."

"We just stopped playing that regularly. Do you know his new song?"

"I just heard it a couple times. 'I Wanna Kiss The Bride,' I think."

"Yeah. What's the number one song in the country?"

"Uh, 'I'll Be Watching You.' It's by Sting. Still hearing it everywhere all summer."

"Close enough. It's 'Every Breath You Take' by the Police."

John looked at his application and said, "Geez, you didn't start working until you were 30? You didn't do a long time in jail for some crap, did you?"

"No. I had a lot of odd jobs here and there and I went to the Morse Center to get some training. I worked at Matt's – a little breakfast and lunch place for three years, but I left there earlier this month when there was a change in ownership. I was assistant manager, and I even supervised a couple of people, but the new man and I disagreed on how to do some things."

"Keith told me how he knows you, and I respect the both of you for that. You don't have any other job?"

"I'm starting work at the mall part-time next week."

The phone rang. John told Ernie to answer it.

"Good morning. Radio 1350. This is Ernie. No. That contest ended yesterday. I'm sorry, but I can't disclose that information. I'll give him that message."

"They hung up," Ernie said to John.

"Very good. That was Keith disguising his voice." They both laughed.

John said, "Keith explained the job to you. I can hire you for Sundays only. We are desperate for somebody we can train part-time to sort of fill in the blanks and help out the DJs and any other staff here. Everybody here is easygoing. We got a deli and a convenience store right nearby so you don't need a car. Keith will be with you for the first couple weeks here. Can you start this Sunday?"

"Sure. I 'll be here at right at 8. Keith said you might be paying $8 an hour?"

John laughed. "Hell, no. Starting DJs make that. Because I'm desperate, I'll start you off at $5.00 an hour and if things work out well, you might get a raise in time for Christmas. I'll get Keith to show you around. Good to have you aboard."

"Thanks, John." They shook hands. Keith came into the office to give Ernie a tour of the station and introduced him to Jim, one of the DJs, and Rex, an employee who had the same work role as Ernie was to have. Rex told Ernie that everyone at the station got along well and he showed him the small room, desk, phone and chair adjacent to the DJs' station.

"You'll be busy. Just don't ever come in late or leave early, no matter what the weather is. You'll be working with Dick and Cindy, the Sunday DJs. Dick has been here for years and he's all business, but if you don't screw up he'll be your friend. Cindy is young, fairly new, and she's a sweetheart. Here's my phone number if you need me."

"He's got my number, too, Rex."

When Midge came home and Ernie told her he got the job at the radio station and the starting salary, she had mixed feelings.

"I'm so glad you'll be working, but on both Saturday and Sunday now? We won't be seeing each other much. I have to see if I can change my schedule to get Mondays and Tuesdays off and work weekends from now on. What are you gonna do Thursdays and Fridays – get another job?"

"I won't have to. With both jobs I'll be making $5000 a year, and that doesn't count any commission I'd be making from selling shoes when it gets busy in a couple of months. That's almost as much as I was making last year. Ask Florence (Midge's supervisor – the head housekeeper at the hotel) if you can get Thursdays and Fridays off. That way I could look for something on Tuesdays – that'd bring it up to $6500 a year. Besides, you'll be getting more tips if you work weekends. We will be OK."

"I'll talk to Florence on Monday," Midge said, resignedly.

Ernie's first day at the radio station was busy, but enjoyable. Dick and Cindy were very helpful. He was tired when he got home, but he thought, "This is gonna work out. Maybe I could train to be a DJ and get an FCC license someday." Luckily, Florence was about to ask Midge if she could change her schedule so she could work at least Saturday or Sunday because of a turnover of staff, and she was pleased to change Midge's schedule starting the following week.

On Wednesday, Ernie arrived at the shoe store just as the mall was opening. Craig introduced him to two of the salespeople, Barbara (the assistant manager) and Tommy – both about in their late 20's - and Karen, a lady about in her mid-40's who was the cashier and who helped out Craig with some of the business duties. Craig took Ernie into the back room where shoes were stacked in boxes high along several walls. Most were women's shoes, but one wall was for men's shoes and another contained children's shoes. Craig started teaching Ernie the stock and code numbers – different codes for women's, men's, and children's shoes, and different code numbers for styles of shoes – all on the shoe boxes. A colored sticker on the box meant that it was an out of style pair, and the sale would bring in extra commission, as well as for selling all handbags and polish (they were in racks near the cashier). Craig pulled out several popular shoes on the walls to demonstrate to Ernie. Then he told Ernie that for the first two weeks he would not be out on the floor selling, but mostly in the back shifting shoes.

"See those gaps in the spaces where boxes were? They have to be tightened up. Don't do it while someone is out on the floor selling that particular pair of shoes – every half hour or so, you have to tighten up the spaces by bringing all the boxes above those shoes where it's empty down so there's no gap between the boxes. If you're not sure where to shift in one place, ask one of us." He demonstrated sandals in a particular style in which a pair of size 7 ½ were sold; shifting would involve bringing down the next box (in this case, a size 8) and all the other boxes on top of them. Fortunately for Ernie the walls were no higher than 6 feet – he wouldn't have to climb a ladder. Ernie told Craig he understood what had to be done.

Craig said, "Look at the shoes and the stock numbers, so you can associate what goes with what. We'll help you. The only time you sit down is if you're in the back or if business is very slow. Once in a while this week and next, hang around the curtain and watch us how we sell to customers – what we say and do. Be polite. You get a half hour for lunch around 1:30. I know you'll have a lot of questions – don't be afraid to ask. Go ahead and start shifting with this wall. It's OK to make small talk with any of us in the back or out front if it's not real busy. You'll meet a couple of part-timers on Saturday. I hope you're not overwhelmed with this information."

"No. If I'm not sure what you want, I'll ask you."

The first two weeks went well. Saturday was busier but he looked forward to his job at the radio station the next day. By the end of the month, Dick told Ernie that he was doing a great job and Cindy would joke back and forth with him when they were off the air. He told Midge that he was exhausted on Sunday night and he would not work anywhere on Mondays, but he would consider working a half day on Tuesdays in October, once he had "routines" down at his workplaces. By the last week of September, he was starting to sell 5 to 10 pairs of shoes per day, and the other employees in the store seemed to like him. Once he had a customer ask, "Didn't you work at the state hospital? Or didn't you used to be a patient there?"

He responded with a smile, "Somebody else asked me that. Apparently, there was a guy named Warren that looks like me."

A couple of people remembered him from the restaurant and he said, "Kenny and I didn't get along, but this is better for me here."

Carol came into the store one Saturday afternoon and bought a pair of dress shoes from him. He had a few minutes to explain what happened to him in the past few years, and he thanked her for the training at the Morse Center. In the meantime, AA was going well, and sessions at the clinic were every three weeks with Arnie. Elaine came by every three weeks on Thursday, and she was phasing out case management visits for them – she was about to see Midge for therapy sessions every two weeks. Midge still went to the Night Club program most Monday nights. Things were going smoothly again for Ernie and Midge for the rest of the fall.

Chapter 24:
A SLOW SELF- DESTRUCTION FOR ERNIE

After Thanksgiving things started slowly changing for Ernie, although Midge continued to do well. Work at the radio station became an oasis compared to the shoe store, where business picked up and Ernie had to take on a few customers at a time on Saturdays. On the one hand, he would get on a hot streak and sell one to two pairs to seven or eight customers in a row, including boots for women (higher priced). But other times he'd forget sizes or bring out the wrong pair of shoes when it got busy. Or he would "walk" (i.e., when a customer wouldn't buy anything and they would leave) 5 or 6 customers in a row, and he would get angry. Once Barbara had to tell him in the back room to "watch your mouth" when after bringing out a total of six pairs of shoes to a customer he just walked, Ernie loudly said as he was going past the curtain into the back room, "She's got a narrow mind to go along with her narrow feet. What the hell does she expect in a (size) 9 AA?"

On another day, he went into the back room and stretched a shoe for a customer, but it ripped. Craig was not happy. He told Ernie, "I know I taught you to stretch shoes and put heel grippers in so they fit, but dammit, be careful. Those were expensive. Fit 'em in their size!" The following Wednesday, Ernie walked a customer and Craig said, "Those are soft leather shoes. Why didn't you stretch them a little?"

"You said, 'fit 'em in their size,' Craig," Ernie frostily responded.

Soon after that, when Tommy was about to approach a man who was looking at a pair of shoes on a rack when 20 feet away, Ernie called out, "Hi, can I help you?" He sold the man a pair, but Tommy went into the back room and said to Ernie loudly, "You son of a bitch, if you ever screw me out of a sale like that again, I'll beat the shit out of you after work!" Barbara came into the back and yelled for Craig, who was in the office. When Craig came and found out what happened, he said to Ernie, "The next time you pull any crap like that, you're fired on the spot! I want you back here shifting shoes for the next hour." Ernie apologized to Craig and Tommy, and things went smoothly after that, although there were times when Ernie seemed irritated with customers. Once a lady asked, "If I don't like these when I wear them out tonight, can I bring them back?"

Ernie responded, "Yeah, but look, the purpose of buying shoes is not to return them. They fit right and they look good on you." She bought the shoes that Wednesday and brought them back Saturday, saying to Karen, "I don't like them. And I didn't like your salesman, either."

Nevertheless, Ernie had a good volume of sales right up through Christmas, which made for higher commission money than he expected. Craig invited him to their holiday party on New Year's Eve (Christmas and New Year's were on Sundays), but Ernie declined, saying he had to work at the radio station early in the morning. Craig understood, but he wasn't pleased. Midge wasn't pleased that they both had to work Christmas day, either. Ernie did get a raise to $5.50 an hour which started on January 1st, just had John had promised.

Craig got drunk at the New Year's Eve party, and this started a week-long binge which culminated in his going into a 28-day rehab program and transferring to another store 35 miles away. Barbara took over as manager of the store, but as usually happens during the first two months of the year or longer in a northern climate, business dropped off greatly. On January 18th, as Ernie reported for work, Barbara called him into her office.

"Ernie, you're a good worker for us, but business is always real slow at this time of year, so I have to lay off you, Jenny and Paul (two young part-timers), starting today. I'm sorry."

"What! You're firing me? Craig never would've done this!"

"I'm not really firing you. It's a layoff. I want to leave things open until around Easter when I might need you back. Or sooner if someone else quits."

"This really screws me, Barb. All I have now is a 1-day a week job. That doesn't pay the bills."

"I hate to be business-like, but it'd cost the store about $3000 paying you for essentially little or no work. I'll give you a reference if you look for another job. Besides, you probably could get some unemployment benefits out of this to help you. Here's where Craig will be in Massachusetts (she wrote down the name and phone number of the store on a piece of paper for Ernie). Call me or stop in here around April 1st."

Ernie turned his back and said, "You didn't have to do this," as he left the store. Midge started crying when he told her what happened later, and said they'd have to live on her income for the most part. She lamented, "That's not fair – you got to get a full-time job, if you can."

The worst was yet to come, though. On the afternoon of the 29th, he was at the radio station when just before 2 o'clock Cindy started getting sick. She told Ernie, "You know how to get on the air. Just play music for the next 15 minutes or so. I have to go to the bathroom now. Call Dick to see if he can come back in, or call Keith."

Ernie looked around as Karma Chameleon by Culture Club was halfway through the song. He thought, "Where the hell is the Elton John album?" Time was running out. He found the Lionel Richie album "Can't Slow Down," and was about to put it on but there was 10 seconds of dead air. Cindy was still throwing up in the bathroom. He saw that it was 2 o'clock and time for the news. He switched to the microphone on the air and impulsively improvised.

"This is Sir Ernie with news, weather, and sports headlines. Reagan announced he is running for re-election as president today. If you want to see who he's running against, take a drive north and check out the ice sculptures of the other guys. In sports, the Pro Bowl is today somewhere out on the west coast. After the Super Bowl last week, only a few people are gonna watch it, so keep listening to us. Weather: snow tonight, snow tomorrow and it's not gonna get much above zero the next day. Here's Lionel Richie – All Night Long."

Cindy came out of the bathroom and said, "You didn't go on the air talking, did you?"

"I had to – it was time for the news. I just did the headlines as best I could."

"Oh, shit! I told you to just play music. Don't ever do that again! If and when Keith and John find out, they're gonna be pissed at us both. You don't have an FCC license – it's illegal."

Ernie said he was sorry, but silently felt it could be his big break to getting on the air as a DJ. Cindy felt a little better physically, but worried about the repercussions of the stunt Ernie pulled. Keith couldn't make it in, but Cindy told him she felt well enough to continue. She asked Ernie to go to the drug store two blocks away for some Pepto-Bismol. Just before Ernie was supposed to go home, Keith called and told him, "I don't know what crap you pulled, but John is furious. He wants you and Cindy on a conference call tomorrow morning at 9 o'clock. You have a lot of explaining to do. Go home now, but let me talk to Cindy." Ernie was wondering if he would still have a job as he gave the phone to Cindy. She was crying as he went out the door – he didn't hang around for her to scream at him. Midge knew something was wrong when Ernie walked in the door.

"I don't want to talk about it. I got to look for another job tomorrow. I might not go back to the radio station. They're getting rid of some people."

"What happened? Tell me!"

"I don't want to talk about it! I don't feel good. I'm going to bed."

The next morning, after a brief discussion of what happened on the air yesterday, John fired Ernie immediately. He told Cindy to give a formal 2-week notice to resign, and he told Keith he was 'skating on thin ice,' and that inevitably the station owners would find out what happened. The upshot of Ernie's caper was that three weeks later John was fired and a new station manager was brought in to transition the station to one of easy listening. Keith, Carla, and Dick were retained as some of the few employees left in this overhaul.

At an AA meeting in February, Keith said to Ernie, "You just about took down the whole station. If John ever sees you again, he might beat the hell out of you. He'd love to try to sue you."

"Ernie responded, "He can't get blood out of a stone. Besides, everything I said in that newscast was true. I'm glad they kept you on."

Keith said, "The more I think of it, maybe the whole situation with the station was a time bomb. I feel bad for Cindy. She'll get another part-time job."

"Can you give me a reference? Or be my sponsor here? Rick moved to Portland last week."

"Hell, no, I can't do either of those things. I can be supportive of you at the meetings here, but nothing else. Good luck finding a job somewhere."

Ernie was able to collect partial unemployment benefits because of the shoe store layoff, but at only about $40 a week. He couldn't find work anywhere through March, and Midge was losing patience with him.

They were getting more irritable with each other. On March 31st, he called Barbara to see if he could come back to the shoe store. She said the store had enough full-time and part-time employees right now, and if ever she needed him, she'd call him.

"Yeah. Thanks, Barb. It's, 'Don't call us; we'll call you.' So much for your promises." He hung up the phone, went out to a local bar where he played pool with some people, lost $20, and got drunk, thinking, "I'm the April Fool a day early."

When Midge came home from work, she was angry. "Ernie, you're destroying yourself. You promised me you wouldn't start drinking again. You're not going to AA much anymore, you cancelled your appointment with Arnie, and you stopped taking your medication. I hope you're not on your way back to the state hospital. What happened that you got drunk today? And you haven't played pool in years and you lost more money?"

"Barbara isn't taking me back at the shoe store. I was banking on that. She says she's got enough people working. Don't bother me. I'm going back to bed."

"I'm the one in this relationship who's doing a lot better. I can run this place where we live. I can manage the finances. I've grown as a person because I got help whenever I needed it. Maybe it's time we broke up. I don't want you being a parasite."

"Shut up! I don't want to hear any of your crap!" He slammed the door to the bedroom and went into their bed with his clothes still on.

Midge started crying, but after a while she called the crisis line, talked with the mental health worker for about 30 minutes and she was in a calmer state. She was contemplating making a decision whether or not to stay there with Ernie or leave. She thought, "I'll always love him, but I can't take this much longer. The rent is paid through April. I have to see Elaine."

Monday was Ernie's birthday. Midge didn't buy him a present, but she brought home a small birthday cake for the two of them. She said she didn't want to go out to eat because money was tight. Ernie was remorseful toward her, but seemed depressed. He smoked a whole pack of cigarettes in the living room (something he hadn't done in a long time) as he blankly stared at their little TV most of the day. He didn't call the clinic or the crisis line, didn't go to any of the AA meetings, and didn't look for work. Midge was irritated at this, but Ernie told her, "Give me a break. Today's my birthday. I'll get out and pound the pavement tomorrow. I know I got to get some kind of job – that's the most important thing. I'll call Arnie and see if he can see me at the clinic. He's the only one I trust there now. I don't want to go back to AA yet, but I will sometime this month."

Ernie couldn't find work for the rest of the month. Leads were flaring up and dying, even at Burger King and Zayre's, a department store in town where they were supposed to be hiring people. Midge was starting to spend more time away from home, sometimes with friends who worked at the hotel, and also with one lady who regularly came to the Nite Club program. Ernie was getting more withdrawn, and depressed. He cancelled an appointment to see Arnie on the 16th. He refused to see Elaine or Arnie for couples counseling, as Midge suggested. He went to an AA meeting during the 3rd week of April, and spoke, but nobody volunteered to be his sponsor. Communication with Midge was becoming strained much of the time, and Midge seemed to think Ernie was becoming a burden. Finally, during the last week of April, after Midge came home from work, she said, "Ernie, we have to talk. We can't go on like this. It's hard for me to say this, but maybe we ought to break up for a while."

"You want to get rid of me? Like you did years ago? You think things are that bad?"

"Yeah. I feel like every day after work, I don't want to go home." She started to cry.

"After all I've done for you, trying to build some kind of life for us! We've kept each other out of the bughouse for years now!"

"It's not the same anymore! Things are so damn tense at home! Look at some of the things you've done in the past six months or so."

"I didn't ask to get laid off at the shoe store! I didn't have any control over Craig getting drunk and leaving! I was trying to help Cindy that day at the radio station! I didn't know Rick was gonna take off and move to Portland! I didn't even know Matt was gonna retire and sell the place!"

"But a lot of it was your fault in the way you reacted. And it's taking a toll on me, but I'm fighting it. And I'm tired of fighting it, and I'm tired of fighting with you. One of us has to leave! I paid the rent this month out of my bank account and I can keep paying it every month. I can buy groceries and cook for myself. I have friends and people who can help me if I need them."

"The hell with you, if that's the way you want it, Midge. I'll be out of here in a few days! If not sooner!"

He grabbed a pack of cigarettes and went outside to smoke, pacing up and down the alley for over an hour. He slept on the couch that night. Two days later, after getting a tip from an AA member at a meeting he attended the night before, he was hired at a diner downtown (same one that shot him down last year) by Cheri, a new manager who knew Matt. Fortunately for Ernie, Cheri knew Kenny and thought he was a jerk. She had an opening for him to start that Monday working 7 a.m. to 11 a.m. as a grill man, making breakfasts only, four days a week. The next day, he also rented a room in a private home, to move in on May 1st. His new residence was within walking distance of work, and like years ago, he would have a tiny refrigerator, a hot plate, some kitchen privileges, and he would be sharing a bathroom with an elderly man who rented another room in the house. Ernie was cautiously optimistic that he was on his way to getting back on his feet again.

Chapter 25:
STARTING OVER

Ernie made an appointment to see Arnie at the clinic on Friday afternoon May 4th, at 4 p.m. He told Arnie about all the recent events that had taken place, and Arnie commented, "You really are resilient. If a cat has nine lives, you have more. Tell me – what happens now?"

"I got to get another part-time job for one day a week, and I got to get a sponsor at AA."

"You'll be picking up the pieces, so to speak, if you do. I don't want to focus on your past so much. I'm more interested in how you see your present and future. But I do want you to tell me what you learned from these recent events."

"I miss Midge already, but I'm starting to think that maybe she and I weren't right for each other after all. She doesn't need me anymore and that hurts. Maybe it's a good thing we never got married. Maybe we need a break from each other. I can't get drunk any more – it comes back to bite me in the ass every time."

"Are you taking your meds?"

"I have to take the Dilantin, or I risk getting seizures. I have some Wellbutrin left. Nothing else. Anything else I take zaps my energy. I learned some good things from Greg James years ago, but one thing he and Jack Orvis said was that everybody needs help sometimes."

"It's Dr. James now. I met him last week at a conference. Your name didn't come up in our conversation, though."

"Is he back at the bughouse?"

"Yeah, but he's leaving for a position in Albany in a few months."

"I'm glad it's Dr. James, but I'd never take a chance on going back to that place even to visit him or anyone else. If you see him again, tell him I said hi."

"Sorry I digressed. Are you going to an AA meeting tonight?"

"Yeah. I'm going to a new place at a church hall. I might not know many people there, but I need a sponsor. I'm gonna ask around. There's just one problem – I don't have a phone right now. Maybe I will if I get a little apartment next year after I save up some money."

The session lasted another 45 minutes, and at the end Arnie provided Ernie with an opinion as to where things stood in his new situation.

"You've been going up and down through tough times since I've known you. This is another adjustment period. You've stayed out of the hospital for years now, and you've been going to the free clinic for a long time for help with your physical problems and your meds. All that is good, but it would behoove you to come to this clinic and keep your appointments. I think we both agree you can't get rid of AA. It's also really important, at your age, that you stay with a job for at least a year or longer. Midge was your major source of stability, personally. You may or may not ever get back with her, but in the meantime, it would help if you can build a core of friends or supportive acquaintances. It's good that you know the ins and outs of the social services system, but you can be more than a mere survivor. Write down a list of what you need to do and bring it in to every session with me and we'll discuss your progress. I'll be out of town all next week, so I'll have to see you in two weeks, but call the crisis line if you have a setback or if things start to go downhill. I'll see you at 3 o'clock on the 18th."

Ernie thanked him and left, thinking, "He's a good guy who really does want to help. He didn't get angry or punitive with me. He's right about everything he said at the end."

At Ernie's new residence, Charlie, a smiling, pudgy, balding 78-year-old man who lived in the room across the hall, was fast becoming Ernie's new best friend. Almost every day they would sit out in the back porch for an hour or two and talk about a lot of their life experiences (Ernie didn't disclose to anyone that he'd been a state hospital from the late '60's through the '70's) while they laughed and smoked a couple of cigarettes.

Charlie openly disclosed his life story to Ernie. He grew up in Worcester, Massachusetts, came to New Hampshire in his early 20's, and got married, but his wife divorced him during the depression years. They had no children and Charlie never re-married. After several jobs with the local fire department and the Boston and Maine railroad, he was drafted when World War II broke out. He was stationed as a Canadian border guard for almost all of his time in the Army, until at the end of the war. Charlie spent his last 25 working years as a clerk in a tobacco shop downtown. He retired late in 1971, just before the store went out of business. He had lots of acquaintances and some friends at the Senior Center downtown, where he hung out several mornings a week. He moved into his present living situation eight years ago when he could no longer afford the rent for the house where he lived for many years (Charlie had no pension; he was surviving on Social Security only). Most of his old friends had passed away.

Charlie enjoyed Ernie's company and they went together to church suppers in town a couple of nights a week. They watched movies and occasionally sports on TV together. Charlie gave Ernie tidbits of advice periodically, based on his life experiences down through the years, and Ernie stook him seriously. He told Ernie, "A lot of life is based on luck, and hardly anything is a sure thing, but admit it when you screw up or overlook something you should've done." Also, "Budget your money. Look for sales and deals when you're buying anything (Ernie already knew that). Pay your bills right away if you can. Financial trouble will stop you in your tracks every time." And, "I stopped drinking a few years after I got out of the Army because I've seen too many guys lose their jobs, lose their homes, and lose their wives or girlfriends because they kept getting drunk. Stay in control of your life or you might lose everything." He enjoyed seeming to take the role of a mentor to Ernie. Ernie was starting to consider Charlie as the father he never really had.

That fall, Ernie eked out a living with his part-time job. He enjoyed his work, living situation, his new AA sponsor (Jake), his sessions with Arnie, and hanging out with Charlie, but he missed Midge and having more independence. Not having a phone was a hinderance – he had to use the phone in the kitchen, and his landlady (who lived upstairs with the same phone line) told him he absolutely could not make any long-distance calls. He had to smoke outside. Plus, the front door would be locked at 10 p.m. every night – no chance of getting an evening or night job for Ernie. The landlady would inspect their rooms and the bathroom once a week to ensure they were kept clean. Although Ernie felt these rules were cumbersome, the rent was cheap and his room and bed were comfortable. Sometimes she gave them leftovers from a dinner when she had company or when she went out with friends at a restaurant. He and Charlie helped each other out with any cleaning chores.

One day in November Charlie returned from the Senior Center and told Ernie that there was a part-time position open at the Senior Center for a few hours on Fridays if he wanted it.

"They'd have you call Bingo, be in charge of the board games, decks of cards, arts and crafts, go around and greet the people, help make soup and sandwiches for lunch, do some light cleaning, and take out the trash. The lady who did it on Fridays passed away last month, and they can't find a volunteer to do this yet."

"I really don't want to volunteer. I'm at the poverty line as it is. Once the first of the year comes, I gotta get a job and maybe even a new place to live."

"I told the Director you'd do it from 10 (a.m.) to 3 (p.m.) for $20.00. You can do all that stuff. Plus, you can sit down a lot instead of standing for 4 hours like you do on your job now, and there's a lot of nice people I can introduce you to. Do you want to do this?"

"I don't know. Let me think about it."

"C'mon, Ernie. Come by the Senior Center after work tomorrow. I'll introduce you to Alice, the Director. Just look around, at least."

"OK, I'll come over."

Ernie went to the Senior Center and when he opened the door, there was Charlie finishing up a game of cards with a few people around a table. Charlie got up and enthusiastically greeted him, introduced him to several people, and brought him over to meet Alice, the Center Director. The interview with Alice went well. After showing Ernie around the premises and going over the requirements for the position, she told him that the job was his, for Fridays only, working 10 a.m. to 3 p.m. for $20 a week, including a free lunch. He agreed, and he was to start the next day, November 16th. As an added bonus, he could help out preparing and serving dinner on Thanksgiving Day the next week instead of Friday (the Center would be closed) and was welcome to have whatever dinner was left at the end of the day. This was an offer he couldn't refuse.

Ernie still did well at his "steady busy" job at the diner, but he thoroughly enjoyed the Senior Center and the people there. He had a great time at the Christmas party and had a couple of ideas for it of which Alice approved. A couple of times people asked him if he was ever a patient on one of the units at the state hospital because he looked and sounded a lot like someone familiar, but he would smile and respond, "I hear that was somebody named Warren. A few people told me I look something like him."

When Ernie woke up on the morning of Christmas Eve, he started thinking about going over to Midge's house because he missed her and maybe she'd take him back. He was pretty sure she might be there because it was a Monday. They had run into each other briefly a couple of times at the clinic, and about seven or eight weeks earlier he said to her, as he was walking away, "I'll always be Midge's Irish." She looked sad, turned away, and went back into the clinic. Ernie stopped, saw her go in the door, and then kept walking home.

He thought, "Things are going OK for me right now, except financially. Arnie said months ago that Midge was my source of stability. I haven't met anyone like her since. I haven't even had a date since I left her. I'm going over there today. But I have to bring her something."

Ernie had a "paint by numbers" kit and one of the patterns was of a boy on a bicycle. It took him over two hours that morning to get the painting the way he wanted, and he painted "Midge's Irish" underneath it. He let it dry for another hour, put it in a manila envelope and went over to see Midge at noon.

She was surprised when she answered the door.

"Ernie, what are you doing here?"

"Can I come in?'

"OK, but only for a few minutes because I'm going out."

"Finishing Christmas shopping?"

"No."

Before she could say anything more, he said, "I got a Christmas present for you."

She opened the envelope, and gave a sad smile and said, "That's sweet, Ernie."

"I missed you so much. Can we get back together? "

She choked up and said, "We can't. I have a boyfriend now. We've been seeing each other for two months and he's driving over to take me out for lunch in a little while. He works as a porter at the hotel."

Ernie felt like a knife went through his heart. In a low voice he said, "He's got a car. I can't compete with that. I'm sorry I bothered you, Midge. I'll always love you."

"I'll always love you, too, but timing is not good right now. I'm falling in love with this guy. I'm sorry."

"Well, Merry Christmas, anyway. Can I at least give you a hug?'

"OK. Merry Christmas."

He limped out the door with his head down, going toward the direction of his living quarters. Midge stood and watched him go away. Ernie went into a bar, got a beer, but then went to the men's room and walked out of the place, leaving a few bills on the counter. He didn't even drink the beer. He went to a phone booth and had a long talk with Jake, telling Jake what happened, but that he was too depressed to drink. He told Jake that he did not want to kill himself, but Jake persuaded him to call the crisis line, anyway. He talked to the crisis counselor for about 20 minutes at a pay phone, and then limped home. He then dropped in across the hall to tell Charlie what happened. Charlie was very supportive and they spent the rest of the evening together, and celebrated Christmas with the landlady and some of her family upstairs. It was comforting to Ernie that he didn't have to spend the holiday season alone. He decided he would make a list of goals that he could accomplish through the next year to make a better, more independent life for himself. He was tired of his life going up and down like the stock market.

Chapter 26:
NEW YEAR, NEW OPTIMISM

Fortunately, Arnie was at the clinic working during the holidays, and Ernie had a session with him on the 28th. After he told Arnie what happened with Midge, they discussed this for a half an hour. Then, with Arnie's non-directive guidance, Ernie started coming up with what he needed to accomplish in the coming year. He liked what he was doing for work, but he needed more hours and more income, and that would not be possible at either place of employment. He came home every day from the diner feeling achy with arthritis flaring up from all the injuries he had years before. At the diner, the only time he could sit was for a five-minute smoke break outside after 10:15 when business slowed down. The Senior Center was five hours without a break, but the work was much more relaxing. There would be no opportunity for more hours there. He would have to get some kind of a desk job for Saturdays, Sundays, or two evenings a week, if that were possible – this would be his main goal. Concurrent with that, for his next goal, he would have to save and budget money enough to get a checking account and possibly even a credit card by the end of the year, neither of which he ever had before.

Another goal would be that if he could save enough money by June, he hoped to move into a cheap studio apartment in town with all or most utilities paid. His present living situation was OK, and Charlie had become a valuable friend, but the years he spent with Midge provided him with more independence, and he missed that. Finally, he needed to make more friends. He had made a lot of acquaintances in the past five years through the jobs he had, AA, and some patients at the clinic. However, Charlie was his only friend, and he wasn't sure if Midge considered him to be a friend anymore. Another girlfriend would be nice, if that could happen. Ernie wanted to try to find opportunities on his own – he knew Arnie would steer him to groups affiliated with the clinic. Making friends with AA people was dangerous because he saw so many of them "fall off the wagon," and he came damn close to doing that on Christmas Eve. For years now, he was conscious that any activity where he might be arrested or in jail would result in him going back to the "bughouse."

Weeks turned into months with no positive changes in his life, but no setbacks, either. At least he was saving some money. He ran into Midge a few times at the clinic and the interactions were pleasant. She even agreed to meet him and Charlie for lunch at a fast-food joint one day in late March, but she made it clear to Ernie that she was still a friend only – nothing romantic any longer. She still had her boyfriend. After Midge left, Charlie told him that she seemed nice and that it was too bad they broke up. Ernie was bummed out for a couple of days, but Alice at the Senior Center invited him over a few afternoons later for cake and ice cream – for his 35th birthday, and others who were celebrating birthdays in April. Ernie was really touched by this – nobody had ever done anything like that for him in his life.

A break came in May. Through a tip from an AA member, Ernie was hired at the same old hotel in town where Midge was employed several years ago to train as a desk clerk one day a week on Sundays. "Drunkards have always come through for me," he thought.

Fred, the elderly manager of the hotel, introduced him to Ruth, a short, thin, 40ish weekend desk clerk. Ernie would be working with her from 7 a.m. to 3 p.m.

She asked, "Weren't you Midge's boyfriend?"

"Yeah, but it's been over with for about a year now."

"Too bad. Sweet girl. But Louise, the head housekeeper, rode her hard. Louise can be a bitch. But you won't have much contact with her. You'll just call over there and give her the room numbers of people who checked out so they can be made up. She'll call back and tell you when the rooms are ready."

Fred said, "We have 50 rooms on three floors. There's no elevator and no air conditioning. You won't be needed to go to any of the rooms unless someone complains about something that needs fixing. Then you'd check it out and call me. I live in the suite on the first floor in #101. Anyway, there's a lot of other things you have to learn. Ruth and I will show you now."

He told Ernie that they didn't have name tags, but he had to wear a decent shirt and tie. He explained how to answer the phone and take messages. "If the guest has a message, call up to the room on the house phone. If they don't answer after three rings, put the message in the box where their room key is stored. Tell that to all guests when they check in. By the way, check out time is at noon. Check in time starts at 2 o'clock. Every room has a 13-inch color TV – no cable - and a clock radio. A few rooms have single beds only. We have a continental breakfast from 7 a.m. to 9 a.m. in that nook over in the corner where those tables and chairs are. One of the housekeepers takes care of that stuff. We have coffee, tea, milk, water, orange juice, bread, butter, a toaster and a couple kinds of donuts. There's a vending machine and an ice machine near the stairway. No soda machine. No cigarette machine. No smoking behind the desk. You get a half hour break in the room in back of the front desk - either at 12 or 12:30 – unless somebody calls for a reservation. 12 to 1 is always a slow time for a Sunday. The parking lot out back has room for about 10 cars – anyone else has to park on the street if the lot is full. Ruth will show you how to check in and check out people, and how to use the credit card slider thing. We take mostly cash or checks from a local or regional bank, but some people pay by Master Card. We don't take any other credit cards. We do have several people staying here who pay on a weekly or monthly basis."

Ruth showed him how to check out guests in the morning. She said, "Be polite. Ask them how their stay was and if there's anything we need to correct. Get their key. Take their payment – here's how to use the credit card thing (she demonstrated), and get some sort of ID if the card looks suspicious, or excuse yourself and call Fred. He's usually here Sunday mornings. Here's how to fill out their receipt (she demonstrated). The copier is over there. Don't argue with them. Like all hotels we get people who were drunk or stoned the night before and they're still dopey when they get out of here. Sometimes there are people who bitch and complain, but this isn't the freakin' Hilton. You can call them an asshole AFTER they go out the door, if you feel that way. Day shift is easier than evenings because you seldom deal with drunks, crackheads or troublemakers. Here's how to take reservations (she pulled out the form, showed him the drawer organized with folders for each day up to 3 months, and demonstrated how to proceed with them). Right after lunch we pull the forms and assign people with reservations to vacant rooms – lower-level ones first. If you have any questions, I'll be here to help. After a month or so, you'll really get the hang of everything. Fred's a good guy. I've been here seven years and he looks out for his employees, but I wouldn't be surprised if this place gets torn down five or six years from now when he retires and moves down south to Myrtle Beach. Hell, this place was built in the early '20's. Oh, and I'll deal with anything the night auditor has for us when he gets off his 11-7 shift."

Work at the hotel went very smoothly and he and Ruth hit it off personally, as well as being work collaborators. Ruth lived alone in a mobile home several miles away. She was divorced with two adult sons – one was living in Syracuse and the other moved to Rhode Island recently. Although she worked Saturdays and Sundays at the hotel, she had a part-time job three evenings a week working at the public library, helping the librarians. Although she was a "take charge" person at work, she minimized Ernie's mistakes in the first month and jumped in to cover for him. She laughed at Ernie's jokes and stories about jobs he had in the past few years (some of which were hard to believe), and she started driving him home from work, even though he had no problem walking and limping several blocks way.

Ruth was becoming more fond of Ernie. In July, she started picking him up at his residence to eat dinner at her house some Monday nights; in return, he would meet her at a theater downtown to treat her a matinee movie the next day. By late August they were getting amorous, but due to their schedules, they couldn't spend the night together. They agreed to avoid getting affectionate at the hotel – Ruth said that if Fred found out, they might get fired. Although Ernie still missed Midge, he thought, "Ruth is the next best thing." Ernie introduced Ruth to Charlie one Tuesday when they were having lunch at a sub shop before going to the movies.

Charlie remarked to Ernie later, "What is she, about 42 or 43? It's good to have an older woman in your life once in a while. I like her, but watch out for her trying to control you – getting you to do things you don't want."

"I like her, and I like working at the hotel, but if I get a full-time job someplace, I bet it'll all come to an end. She's not Midge, but I'm enjoying the ride so far."

"I hope you won't give up the Senior Center."

"I would try to fit in volunteering there somehow, if I'm working full time."

In fact, he was helping out Alice very well on Fridays as a "jack of all trades" person at the Senior Center, but she couldn't hire him for more hours. The job at the diner was getting monotonous, although staff and customers appreciated him. Some of his sessions with Arnie included stating things assertively instead of aggressively when Ernie didn't like certain procedures. Any complaints or suggestions that he made at the diner were usually to Cheri near the end of the shift; in the first three hours of work, he was steadily busy. At the hotel, there were a couple of times he became smart-mouthed with guests when they told him he didn't know what he was doing when they asked him to fix their TV (for example), or when they had a problem with the room they reserved, or their bill at checkout. Ruth usually jumped right in to defend him and once they had to call Frank when a guest threatened Ernie. Another time, in September, a guy who was still slightly drunk when he was checking out started accusing Ernie of being a former state hospital patient who ripped him off on a World Series pool scam 10 years ago. Ernie was initially taken aback - he didn't remember the guy at all, but he vaguely remembered making money in a shady deal there betting against the Red Sox in '75. He vehemently denied he did any such thing and the man started ranting that, "You let crazy people run this place! I'll tell everybody I know never to set foot in here again!" Ernie was slightly unnerved and walked into the back room saying, "He's the one who should be up there at the bughouse." Ruth did a good job covering for Ernie and got rid of the customer at check out.

This incident bothered Ruth. Later, as he got in her car and she drove him home, she asked him if he were ever a patient at the state hospital.

"Yeah. I was down on my luck years ago and I tried to kill myself. I jumped off a building. That's why I walk with a limp and have all these aches and pains. I take meds for seizures. Please don't ever tell Fred about it."

"Were you drunk? You never want any beer or wine when you're over at the house. What happened to you?"

"I don't want to talk about it. My drinking days are over."

"I can't have you over tomorrow night. I have to go into the library. One of the people is on vacation and they need me to cover."

"OK. I'll see you next Sunday."

Ruth thought, as she drove away, "We have to cool it socially. My ex-husband threatened to kill me and kill himself years ago. I'll meet him for lunch or dinner, but no more coming over to my place or going to movies. This is gonna be uncomfortable on Sundays now."

After he got home, Ernie thought, "I should've lied. Nobody else but Midge knows about my past. Not even Charlie. I don't want to quit the hotel. What if she tells Fred – she didn't say she wouldn't do that. He'll get rid of me. Can we break up and still work together?"

The next week was routine for Ernie. On Saturday afternoon, he went for a walk in the park nearby with Charlie and he told him that things with Ruth were probably coming to an end.

"I didn't think it would last with the two of you. Did she get too controlling?"

"I'll just say I realized we're not right for each other. I still miss Midge."

"You still have to work with her, though. Maybe you can meet some younger girl. They have some ads to meet people in that weekly newspaper."

"I don't drive and I don't have my own place. Hell, I don't even have my own phone anymore."

"Maybe it's time for you to move on with your life – get a steady full-time job and your own place. I'd hate to see you leave the house, though."

"I think you're right, but I love it at the Senior Center."

"Too bad Alice doesn't have anything full-time open for you."

"I'm putting away money, but I don't have enough to move out. Starting next week, I have to try to get a full-time job."

He didn't sleep well Saturday night. Neither did Ruth. They went about their work with no incidents; the mood seemed one of contrived friendliness and more businesslike than usual. At the end of the shift when they got outside, Ruth said that she'd like to go to Mc Donald's with him. "We have to talk."

They got cups of coffee and sat in a booth near the window. They were the only people there.

Ruth spoke first and related what happened with her ex-husband and said to Ernie, "I don't know how to say this to you, but the thought of anyone who would make a serious suicide attempt is chilling to me. I don't think you're crazy, though."

"Thanks, Ruth. I don't think we should see each other socially anymore. That can complicate things at work. I was nervous today. I'm glad I didn't screw up anything."

"I hope we can still work together. I'm glad you understand."

"You didn't tell Fred, did you?"

"No. Like I said before, he'd fire us. So you better be nice to me," she laughed.

That seemed to break the ice. They agreed to try to go back to the way things were before they were involved. Ruth said, "If it doesn't work, I'll ask Fred to move me to the 3 to 11 shift."

Things went better on Sundays after that, but Ernie still felt as if there were a sword over his head if anyone "found him out," given some of the shaky characters that came into the hotel on Saturday night and check out Sunday morning. He tried to look for a full-time job when he could, but to no avail. He was stuck with three part-time jobs, but he had enough money saved to open a checking account and move into a small apartment by the end of the year. Charlie declined his offer to move in with him, but he encouraged him to become more independent. Jake told him that if he got a new place to live to make sure he got his own phone, because someone moving into a new place alone might have a temptation to drink over the holidays.

On the afternoon of December 13th at the Senior Center, Alice called him into her office and told him she had a vacant position. She offered Ernie a full-time job there to start on Monday, December the 29th. He would be supervising a couple of volunteers in the kitchen, take part in some of the other activities at the center, and be a member of the Center's activity planning committee. It would be a 40-hour work week, Monday through Friday, 8 a.m. to 4:30 p.m. He would have two weeks' vacation, holidays off, three personal days, seven sick days, and health benefits. He would start at $7.50 per hour with a raise to $9.00 per hour provided he passed a successful 6-month probation period.

Ernie loudly responded, "Yes, Yes!" This was the biggest promotion of any kind in his life. After discussing some details and filling out some paperwork, he asked Alice if he could give her a hug – he had tears in his eyes. She said, "OK," with a smile on her face. She would announce his hiring at the Christmas party the next Friday. This was one of the happiest days of his life. He was "walking on sunshine" as he trudged through the streets back to the rooming house and when he told Charlie, they went out to a nearby restaurant for dinner to celebrate. On Sunday and Monday, he gave his two-week notices to quit his other part-time jobs. After work on Sunday, he got the newspaper and started looking for one room apartments downtown. On Thursday, he found a partially furnished studio apartment two blocks away from the Senior Center. There was a security deposit and a 6-month lease, but heat was paid for. He would have to pay for electricity and he would have to get a phone. He would move in on January 2nd. He thought, "All's well that ends well. If I count Ruth as one, I accomplished all my goals for 1985."

Chapter 27:
CAN ERNIE SUSTAIN SUCCESS?

After Ernie got his first paycheck, he bought a Queen-sized bed, a dresser, a table and a lamp from a discount furniture store. He ordered a small TV from Ames department store, and he arranged for everything to be delivered to his new apartment. While he was at Ames, he bought some pots and pans, plates and flatware, a few towels, pillows, pillowcases and sheets, and some cleaning supplies. Charlie helped him pick out some of the purchases, and took him to the local thrift shop to buy some clothes. His first two weeks on the job went well, but after the first committee meeting, he proposed a flurry of ideas to add to the routine, some of which were unconventional – such as challenging people from another Senior Center in a town 20 miles away to a day-long tournament of various games ("but they would have to travel here."). Alice pulled him aside after the meeting, and suggested that he do more listening than talking in future meetings until he understood the business and logistics of the Center better. He volunteered to help compile statistics for certain operations of the Center, and a member of the Board of Directors said he was amenable to Ernie helping him.

Ernie wanted to see if he could drive a car and maybe get a license, and in early March he convinced Jake to meet him after work and go to an empty high school parking lot to try. But after five minutes, he knew the poor functioning in his right foot and leg from the chronic injuries years ago would never let him operate any vehicle other than a bicycle competently. He felt bummed out by this; Jake felt sorry for him and bought him dinner before he went to the AA meeting. At least he saved up to buy a good second-hand Schwinn a few weeks later, as the weather started to improve. He could safely lock it up in the back of the apartment building where a couple of other tenants also stored bikes.

Ernie had made some acquaintances over the past several years, but Charlie was his only friend. He hadn't had a date since Ruth back in October, and he thought this might be a good time for pursuing female companionship. He decided to call Midge; he hadn't seen her since one brief encounter a few days after Thanksgiving at the clinic. There was no answer, so he thought that he would ride over to her place late one Sunday afternoon. He knocked on the door and Midge soon appeared.

"Ernie. Hi. I didn't expect to see you. Are you OK?"

"Yeah. I just wanted to talk to you for a few minutes. I tried to call you yesterday and got no answer. Can I come in?"

"I got a few minutes but I'm going out in about a half an hour. What's up?"

Ernie proceeded to tell her about many of the good things that have happened to him in the past four months. She said that she was happy for him, but good things were happening for her, too. Then she flashed an engagement ring on her left hand.

Ernie's smile disappeared and his heart sunk. "I was hoping maybe we'd get back together now that I'm in the best period of my life," he said, sadly.

"We haven't set a date yet, but it's probably gonna be in the fall."

"The same guy who works at the hotel with you?"

"Yeah. We decided we don't want to have kids because of problems with depression and anxiety I've had all my life and he's had a grandmother and sister who were psychotic and wound up in the state hospital."

"Back when we were together, we thought we couldn't deal with the stress of kids."

"The other thing is, we'll stay here in this area. I'm learning to drive and I hope to get a car of my own this year."

"I can't drive because of my right leg and foot. I tried to practice last month."

"That's too bad, but I'm glad everything's going well for the both of us. We'll always be friends. I'll always care. Why don't you come back to the Nite Club at the clinic?"

"I'll think about it. I'm still seeing Arnie once a month. I've gotta go, Midge. I'll see you around."

"Maybe I'll see you at the clinic."

"If I don't, I wish you good luck and happiness. I'm in the phone book if you ever need me."

Ernie sped away on his bike and almost got in an accident on the way home. He thought about seeing or calling Charlie, but instead he went right home, watched TV for a few hours (not eating dinner) and he went to bed. He thought for a few minutes, "If this wasn't Sunday night, I'd go out drinking. No bars are open now, though." He thought about calling Jake, but he went right to sleep by 8:30.

Ernie quickly showed signs of struggling after that. He lost some weight and was even more thin than usual. At work he occasionally seemed irritable and snappy toward the volunteers. He called in sick a couple of times in a six-week period. He shouted down one of the seniors in an argument over who won a bingo game. He was silent unless spoken to in his monthly committee meeting, and sat in the corner of the table with his arms folded. He went to AA meetings, but declined to speak to the group when Jake asked him, saying that he wasn't feeling well. Ernie didn't tell Jake he was fighting off the urge to drink, but Jake started to call him every few evenings because he sensed something was bothering him. Ernie cancelled an appointment with Arnie. His only confidant was Charlie, who knew everything taking place in his life. Charlie was concerned and he told Alice. Alice was sympathetic, but firmly stated to Ernie in mid-May, "You better lose the attitude because your probationary evaluation is coming up soon. I know once in a great while you get into these moods for a day or so, but they haven't lasted for weeks since I've known you."

"OK. I'm sorry, Alice. I won't bring my outside life into work. Life goes on."

"Maybe you should see a counselor or therapist."

"I have a guy I've been seeing for a while now. I have to see him Thursday when I get off work."

"We want you to succeed, Ernie, but it's up to you."

Ernie told Arnie everything that happened, and Arnie took the approach, "You can't rewind and do life over, so let's go over whatever your choices are toward living a happier life."

"That's just it. I've never been able to stay happy for more than a few months at a time. I thought I would live happily ever after if I never went back to the bughouse and stayed with Midge."

"In your 36 years on this earth how many people do you know that are happy and joyful every single day for years and years? Happiness is relative. All people get into good periods, but there are always problems, unexpected bad breaks, 'dammits,' 'aw shits,' and the like that people try to overcome. You, of all people, should know that. Ask yourself, 'What happens now? What choices do I have? Have I made good decisions in the past toward improving my life from setbacks?' You are a resilient guy. A lot of guys who went through what you did would've been dead 10 to 15 years ago."

"I've heard stuff like this before from Greg and I have to convince myself of all that, and it isn't always easy. Right now it still hurts because of Midge. That was the trigger. At least I didn't get drunk or lose my job."

"What choices do you have with Midge?"

"Hardly any. She's willing to be friends, but anything other than small talk with her is probably gone. I'll see if I can find a new girlfriend. Will I ever meet anyone like her that was as right for me? You never know."

"I want you to think about what you can do to find some female companionship, if you think you're ready for that. You probably need more of a support system. Think about whether or not you need meds other than Dilantin, which I see you're taking now. Wellbutrin is one good anti-depressant you probably never had, but I can't prescribe it and it's up to you whether or not you feel you need something like that."

"I had it before for a little while. I'd rather wait on that one."

"OK, I'll see you in two weeks. When you come back, I want you to write down three good things that have happened, and five good things about yourself."

Things were relatively better for Ernie after that, with two exceptions: Alice, erring on the side of caution, decided to keep him on probation for another six months, and he wasn't able to meet anyone he could date right through the summer. He went to the movies and to the mall mostly alone and took buses instead of his bicycle. Charlie was declining in health and outside of work, Ernie saw him a couple of times a week, at most. He went to AA meetings a few times a week to be around some people in his peer group, and he met Jake for a late Saturday morning breakfast every couple of weeks. Sessions with Arnie were going well; Ernie decided that he did not need any antidepressant meds. Nothing bad was happening in his life, and he felt better about himself as a person, but pangs of loneliness flared up within him once in a while.

His social life perked up a little in late September. He saw an ad in the weekly newspaper for a support group dealing with people who have experienced debilitating injuries that met Tuesday evenings downtown. He decided to show up at this meeting, thinking, "What have I got to lose? I can tell my story but I won't say it happened at the state hospital – just that I fell out of a 4th story window. I can be vague about the rest." Six people were there, including a counselor (rehabilitating from a car accident) who worked at Second Chance House - the place that had rejected Ernie years earlier. She didn't know Ernie. Just before Ernie spoke, a thirtyish, wiry built guy named Mike told his story of making a suicide attempt by jumping several floors inside a hotel lobby. He miraculously survived, leaving him with a badly broken arm and leg and brain damage, which affected his speech. He spent six months in the same state hospital unit where Ernie had been. Ernie didn't admit to ever being in the state hospital (he was still paranoid of the stigma), but he started to befriend Mike, who lived in a local group home. Mike freely talked about being in the state hospital and living in a group home. Ernie's questions to him after and before sessions in the next few weeks about these ("Do they really do…?") and comments ("I hear the nurses in that place…) made for interesting interactions between them. It appeared Ernie was making a new friend. They met each other for lunch and watched a couple of college football games together at Ernie's place that month. The group grew to nine people within a month, but Ernie didn't feel he had much in common with anyone else until a new lady about Ernie's age came into the group in mid-November.

Her name was Diane. She lived about a half mile away from Ernie in an apartment building, and she was a secretary at a local bank downtown. She was a passenger in a car with another female friend going home from a night of bar hopping and dancing a year earlier when they were hit by a drunk driver, who was killed. Her friend recovered from her injuries and moved away several months ago. Diane's case against the insurance company was still in litigation. She was walking with a 4-pronged cane, but was able to work – she enjoyed her job. She had a 15-year-old son, but her husband won custody of him as a result of their divorce in 1984. Her son wanted to live with his father, who was the leader of a prominent rock band now based in Hartford.

Ernie, after the meeting, asked her if she ever considered going to AA and told her that he was a member and had a good sponsor.

Diane said, "I've considered it from time to time. I start drinking when I feel depressed, but I never lost time from work because I was too hung over. I don't drink alone, or in the morning. My boss and some of the other people at work are real supportive. I saw a shrink for several months and she helped. I hardly ever get to see my son. Both of my parents are dead. I have a sister with a family in North Carolina. I see them at Christmastime. You've been walking with a limp for a long time?"

"Yeah – many years. I can't drive because of it. I'd love to talk to you longer, maybe have lunch or dinner this weekend, but you probably got a man in your life."

Diane was momentarily taken aback, and she asked, "What kind of work do you do?"

"I run the kitchen at the Senior Center, and I help out with a lot of other things. I'm the caller for Bingo and I give out the games and cards."

"Do you know Margaret Dansereau?"

"Sure, I know Marge. She sits at the table with my friend Charlie. Nice lady."

"She's my aunt. Tell you what, I'll meet you at the Crown for an early dinner Saturday, say 4:30."

"Upscale. I've never been there. I can't do any drinking."

"That's OK. I won't drink. We'll go Dutch."

The dinner went well. Diane told him she wasn't looking for any kind of steady, exclusive romantic relationship, but for some companionship once in a while, or someone for phone conversations once in a while. This was fine with Ernie. He told her all about himself, except that about his late teens through his twenties he said they were not good years for him because he "drifted from job to job – all temporary and boring, like at a bookbindery, for one." But he admitted that he was seeing a therapist at the clinic and that the job at the Senior Center for the past year was the best steady position he ever had in his life. He told funny stories about the other jobs he had. She laughed hard about what he did at the radio station. They saw each other in the group for the next few months (the group ended in February) and every few weeks for a date. She would pick him up at his apartment. They kissed goodnight at the end of each date. They called each other twice a week. He continued to see Charlie, at the rooming house occasionally. Charlie was going to the Senior Center only a couple of days a week now because he was starting to deteriorate physically. After the group ended, he and Mike talked on the phone once every few weeks, but they didn't see each other all winter. Ernie got off probation at work in January and things were going very well there, as they were in most other areas of his life.

The rest of 1987 through the first part of 1988 was the most relatively uneventful period in Ernie's life. With encouragement from Diane, he cleaned his apartment and did his laundry every few weeks. They started spending the night at each other's places about once a month after going to a movie. He had a conflict with some noisy upstairs neighbors periodically, but they moved out in six months after being evicted by the landlord. Others in the building had complained about their periodic arguing, drinking, and the smell of marijuana. He saw Charlie twice a week at the rooming house. Charlie was going to the Senior Center only about once a week now. He went to AA meetings two to three nights a week with Jake picking him up and driving him home. Ernie had over 3 ½ years of sobriety – the longest he had been sober in 15 years. He was handling his checking account well, and opened a savings account as a 38th birthday present to himself. He was seeing Arnie at the clinic only once a month now, mainly for support for continuing and strengthening the lifestyle of a "normal" human being. At times he felt like what Arnie told him was an "imposter syndrome," i.e., believing that his run of success was mainly luck and "too good to be true." At this point in his life, things were going great for Ernie.

Chapter 28:
A DOWNHILL SPIRAL

As winter turned into spring, Ernie had experienced intermittent arthritis from all the injuries he encountered at the state hospital many years before. Changes in the weather, especially to cooler, rainy days, were irritating joints in various areas of his body more often and he started taking Advil and Anacin at times to dull the pain. He was tempted to drink whiskey, but he knew this would bring on a downhill slide. He didn't think he could afford to see a physical therapist. There were days when he wanted to call in sick, but he "toughed it out" because he knew there were a lot of people at the Senior Center 40 years older than him who showed up regardless of their aches and pains. Some mornings the pain in his right leg throbbed when he was riding his bike. He couldn't wait for warmer weather to come.

But as the temperatures outdoors rose in May, Diane started to see him less often, giving Ernie various excuses. She had an answering machine, but she stopped returning his calls. When he went over to her place one night in late June, she said through the door that she "had company, and I'll call you tomorrow night." She didn't call, so he called her at 10 o'clock. Diane answered, and told him, "Ernie, I'm sorry, but I can't see you anymore. For two months now I've been seeing this new guy from work who's a branch manager of the bank. I'm falling in love with him, and he wants me to move in with him. He's here tonight. I'm so sorry."

"I'm sorry, too," Ernie quickly responded, as he slammed down the phone.

After angrily pacing through the house and cursing for about 15 minutes, he put on his shoes, grabbed his wallet, and limped to a local bar three blocks away. He sat alone in the corner of the bar and in one hours' time, he drank three Jim Beam and waters before he staggered out of the bar and limped home. He called in sick the next day, and, feeling remorse, called Jake that afternoon.

"Why didn't you call me last night?"

"I was pissed off at the world. I've been in pain, physically, anyway."

"You know that's not the right way to deal with this. Anyway, so you slipped up. Don't beat yourself up. Just call me first. That's what I'm here for. I'll pick you up at six and we'll go to the meeting at the church hall tonight."

For the next month, it was "back to normal" for Ernie. While he was at work on Friday, July 30th, Alice called him into her office just as he finished calling the numbers for the daily Bingo game.

"Ernie, please sit down, I just got some bad news. You know that Charlie wasn't doing well physically for a while now, right?"

"Yeah. Is he in the hospital?"

"He was rushed to the hospital last night. He had a stroke and passed away this morning. I'm so sorry. All of are really gonna miss him. He was such a good man."

Ernie slumped in his chair and started to weep, saying, "He was the best friend I ever had. I learned so much from that old guy."

Alice hugged him and told him he could take the rest of the day off. "You and I and some other people can plan for some kind of celebration of life event here soon. Charlie would've liked that and a lot of people here will really miss him."

"Thanks for telling me, Alice. I'll go home. Can I leave my bike here? I'd rather walk home."

"I'll call you as soon as I hear details about the wake and funeral."

"I'll see you Monday."

Ernie limped home and called Arnie, but he had left for the weekend. He felt the urge to get drunk again, but this time he called Jake who came right over to his place and spent a couple of hours with him before they went out to dinner and to an AA meeting. After the meeting, Jake drove Ernie home and said, "I'm on call for you on speed dial all weekend. Don't hesitate if you need me. If you can't get a hold of me, call the crisis line."

Amazingly, Ernie made it through the weekend without drinking and he only called Jake three times. He had some trouble sleeping and eating. It was a sad day at work on Monday when Alice told the group that the wake was tonight and that Charlie would be cremated. There was no memorial service, but the Senior Center planned for a Celebration of Life for the following week. Ernie was bummed out for the whole month of August. He went to the AA meetings with Jake a few times; he told Jake he was too depressed to drink. He saw Arnie who talked to Ernie about grief and the grieving process, and he encouraged Ernie to come back to the Nite Club program. Ernie was reluctant to do this because Midge was no longer there and he didn't want anyone to remind him of the years he had spent in the state hospital.

But Arnie was the focus of another shock for Ernie right after Labor Day. He told Ernie that he was taking a position as Director of a small mental health clinic in Maine starting October 3rd and that his last working day here would be September 30th. Ernie was stunned at first, and then he was angry.

"You give me all this crap about a support system and this summer I've lost my girlfriend, my best friend and now the therapist I've had for years!"

"You can build it back up again. You've made a lot of contacts with people since I've known you. You still have your AA sponsor and your job. I'm sorry for you that I'm leaving but Elaine is still here and she is willing to be your therapist. She'll be taking over most of my caseload."

"I don't want to see Elaine. She was better for Midge than me."

"I can see you again next week, same time."

"No, schedule me for your very last day, same time. Maybe I'll come in; maybe I won't."

Ernie got up and left. He stopped into a liquor store on the way back and bought a fifth of Old Grand Dad. He stayed in his apartment and drank on and off the whole weekend. On Sunday late in the afternoon, he threw out what was left in the bottle, took a nap, and called Jake as he fought off a hangover, telling him that "I did something stupid," and he related his tale of frustration to him.

Jake responded, "Ernie, you do things out of anger. It's like the guy who hits first and asks questions later. I'll come over and we'll go to a meeting tonight."

"No. I threw out the rest of the bottle. I promise you I'll go to the meeting tomorrow night. I'll get up and talk, maybe. I have to get in condition to go to work tomorrow. You and the job are all I have left right now."

"Re-read the 12 Steps. Good thing it's Sunday night. If you need me, PLEASE call me. I'll pick you up tomorrow night at 6:30."

Ernie made it to work on time. He told Alice that he had "a bad weekend," but he didn't want to discuss it with her. But he promised to do the best job he could. All day long people sensed that he was not his intermittently jovial self. Near the end of the day at work, he got a call from Elaine, and he responded loudly, "No, I am NOT going to see you or anyone else there until further notice!" He hung up the phone. Alice called him aside and asked, "Ernie, what was that all about?"

He asked if he could talk to her for a minute in her office. They went in and he closed the door.

Ernie said, "All I can tell you is something you might have already found out about me. I'm in AA – I've been going to meetings for years, sometimes even three or four times a week. I hope you won't hold it against me. I have a sponsor who's a good guy and we're going to a meeting tonight. I've never shown up for work drunk or smelling like booze, or hung over, even though I've slipped up a few times and this weekend was one of them."

"Who was that on the phone?"

"That was a nurse at the mental health clinic. She used to see me and my ex-girlfriend for sessions a few years ago. I was seeing a psychologist at the clinic and he's leaving there. He wanted to transfer me to her. You're not gonna get rid of me, are you?"

"No, you're doing a good job. Just try as hard as you can to leave your personal life at home and don't let it affect your work here. Why didn't you ever tell me this?"

"It's confidential. Keep this to yourself, but this year, I had a girl-friend break up with me, I lost Charlie – you know he was a very close friend even before I started here, and now this counselor is leaving."

"Really, you should get some professional help if you need it. It's good that you're in AA, but if you come to work here impaired or if you're not performing your duties well, I may have to suspend you or let you go. I'm glad you told me this, but I'll give all the support I can here. Just don't self-destruct on me."

"I won't. Thanks, Alice."

The rest of the year was better for Ernie. He didn't go to the clinic again, but he went to AA meetings with Jake three times a week. There was a new younger guy in AA, Sam, who got Ernie interested in learning chess (Sam was a novice player) and they would play Saturday mornings in a room at the library downtown until one Saturday morning Sam didn't show up. Apparently, Sam got drunk at a party the night before, destroyed the place, and wound up in jail. At times Ernie would go to movies alone at the mall; there were no ladies on the horizon who he could date. Jake invited him to his house for Christmas dinner, and since he knew Ernie was lonely, he called him twice on New Year's Eve. Ernie's job was still enjoyable, and he received a good evaluation and a small raise from Alice at the end of the year.

In late February more bad news surfaced for Ernie. Alice's husband got a major promotion with his company and he and Alice were moving to North Carolina at the end of March. Ernie was not only sad to see her leave, but he was experiencing anxiety every day at work because no candidate to replace her was hired by the Board of Directors by the time Alice left. With Jake's help and AA meetings, he fought off the urge to drink. Jake also smartly encouraged him to get a letter of recommendation from Alice before she left, which Alice was pleased to do. A Board member who was a retired social worker agreed to be the Interim Director until a new person was hired.

In late April, a nurse who had spent 25 years working on the Medical/ Surgical unit of the state hospital was hired. Her name was Doris, and when she was introduced to Ernie, she was taken aback. Ernie had a shocked look on his face. This was a nurse with whom he had several arguments 10 years earlier when he was a patient on her unit.

An hour before lunchtime, Doris called Ernie into her office. She said, "Sit down. I remember you. Your name isn't Ernie, it's Warren and you were a patient in the state hospital for a long time. Did you con somebody to get this job?"

Ernie angrily responded, "My name is W. Ernest LeBlanc and no, I didn't con anybody to get this job. I resent what you said. I've been working here for 2 ½ years and I've been out of that damn place up there for nine

years. I've had food service training at the Morse Center, supervised someone when I worked at a restaurant and got two good evaluations since I've
been here. I've come a long way, baby!"

"You don't call me 'baby.' There will be some changes at this Senior
Center. I'll be watching you and a few other people who work here. Get
back to work. I'll be eating lunch here today."

Ernie stormed out of Doris' office and went back to the kitchen. He
told a volunteer there that he had to go outside to smoke a cigarette, and
he'd be back in to make sandwiches and salads in a few minutes. As he
smoked the cigarette, he thought, "I wish I could put something in her food
to give her diarrhea. But then she'd fire me on the spot. Of all the damn bad
luck I have, with this bitch now running the place."

Lunch went off well. Doris said nothing to him for the rest of the
day. Ernie was too upset to call the numbers for Bingo (one of the volunteers did it), and instead went with some of the people on a shopping trip
to the mall. He called Jake as soon as he got home, telling him of his bad
day at work, and that he had the urge to drink. Jake picked Ernie up at his
place and they went to an AA meeting, and afterwards had a long talk at a
McDonald's. He advised Ernie to go through the motions of work, do his
job, avoid Doris as much as he could, stay silent in the committee meeting, and start using a personal day or two to look for another job. Also,
he suggested that Ernie go to AA meetings more often, and to call him
every evening.

For the next month, Ernie dreaded going to work, and one of the
Seniors remarked to him that it seemed like he was walking on eggshells
lately. A rumor started spreading that he "was a crazy man who got out of
the state hospital and was working there under another name." The older
people who came to the Center didn't believe it; the newer people didn't
seem to trust Ernie.

At the end of May, Doris called a meeting of all staff. She said that
after meeting with the Board of Directors recently, resources had to be

reallocated and the Center's money had to be spent differently. A few positions would be eliminated, and the Center would rely more on volunteers, nursing students and occupational therapy students. She would supervise the nursing students, and a part-time recreation therapist would supervise the OT students. A catering service would provide all lunches and meals for parties. The kitchen would be used only for special events by occupational therapy students and volunteers for cooking classes, with some of the seniors coming to the center helping. For those whose positions would be eliminated, June 30th would be their last working day, and effective immediately their hours would be cut to 20 per week.

Ernie yelled out, "No!"

Doris said she wanted to see him in her office after the meeting. Ernie stormed out and went outside to smoke a cigarette and he paced. He came back inside and the meeting had just ended. Immediately he went to Doris' office.

She said to him as she entered, "Close the door."

Ernie slammed the door and screamed, "Why are you firing me? I've done a good job here for the past few years!"

"Don't you yell at me or I will fire you right now! Technically, I'm not firing you. For the Center to provide better services, given our financial situation, I had to eliminate a few positions and one was yours. I'm sorry you're upset about it, but the Board of Directors approved this."

"Yeah, right! You never liked me from years ago. You're not giving me any credit for turning my life around. I'm not the same person I was 10 years ago, but I see that you still are. You don't have to get rid of me."

"You still have a month left to work here. I gave you more than fair notice. Maybe next year if the changes don't work out and we have a position open, you'll be given due consideration if you apply to come back here."

"For me and the couple of other people you're doing this to, it's on your conscience – if you have one." He limped out of her office and went home. Fighting off the urge to go to a bar and a liquor store, he called Jake and told him he really needed to see him ASAP before he went out and got drunk. Jake was leaving work himself and he drove over to Ernie's place. They talked for an hour.

Ernie tearfully told him what happened and he said, "You and AA are all I got now."

Jake told him, "Ernie, don't quit or do anything else to get fired. This is really a layoff. What this means, by eliminating your position, is that you can get unemployment benefits next month. In fact, you can probably get unemployment for up to a year if you can't find a job. All you have to do after you file for unemployment is go out and look for work at least once a week. Your checks will start coming to you about a month after you file. In the meantime, you'll have enough money to survive, hopefully."

"Dammit, this is the best job I've ever had. I probably won't get anything this good ever again."

"You don't know that. In the meantime, it hurts, but you have to play her game until June 30th when you're out of there. Don't do anything to piss anyone off there. Do you have any leave time coming?"

"I have a week and one personal day, and a couple of sick days."

"It's up to you to decide how you use the leave time - get paid for it or use it all up if you can't stand it there. In the meantime, it'd be a good idea to go back and find another therapist at the clinic. I can only do so much. But let's go to the AA meeting at the church now."

"Thanks, Jake," Ernie sadly said.

After the meeting, Jake drove Ernie home and as Ernie got out of the car, Jake said, "One last word of advice: Bite your tongue and apologize to her. Again, stay out of her way unless you can't avoid her until you're out of there at the end of the month. And again, go to as many AA meetings as you can. This is a dangerous time for you right now."

LIFE LIKE A SEE SAW

Ernie took Jake's advice and followed it exactly. He used his personal days and called in sick twice over the next three weeks, but saved his leave time because he would need the money. One of the people at AA heard his story and said that maybe he could file an EEOC complaint, but Jake suggested he not consider this unless he were still unemployed by the end of the year. On his last day, after calling the Bingo game and announcing that it was his last day (which most of the Seniors knew), the members clapped and cheered for him. Some gave him cookies, muffins, and cupcakes to take home when he went around shaking hands at the end of the day. Doris left work during the Bingo game and left a note for Ernie stating that his last paycheck and reimbursement for leave time would be mailed to him some-time in mid-July. She did not thank him for his service.

Ernie filed for unemployment. Unfortunately, his checks were for only $78 a week since Doris cut his work hours for the last month, and there were no jobs available that summer wherever Ernie looked. However, he got an appointment to see a counselor at the clinic, Stu, who he recognized as a voice from a lengthy call he made to the crisis line years ago. They quickly developed a positive rapport. Stu arranged for him to see the new psychiatrist, Dr. Brennan, and she subsequently changed Ernie's medication from Phenobarbital to Tegretol. Stu suggested he come to a Wednesday evening group starting August 2nd that a new vocational guidance counselor was trying to get started. Ernie was disappointed that the group disbanded after a few weeks, and after the last session he found out that it was probably too late for him to file an EEOC Complaint against Doris, but he did get valuable information regarding how to properly construct a resume, the importance of letters of recommendation, and to never list a job on a resume shorter than six months unless there was a promotion. Still, even though unemployment in the region was low, he couldn't catch a break when he tried to get hired as a cook at a restaurant, or as a desk clerk at a hotel or motel, or as an activity aide at nursing homes. He still felt that working at one of the fast-food places would be a step backward for him. Ernie kept going to AA meetings, and kept in touch with Jake regularly, who took him to three meetings a week. At times he felt like getting drunk, but he couldn't afford it financially, physically, or mentally. Ernie was back to being "marginal man" again.

One Saturday in mid-September, Ernie took a bike ride to a downtown park. He stopped to smoke a cigarette and gaze out at the Merrimack River for a few minutes. As he was about to get back on his bike, a lady slowly pulled up to him in an old Toyota and beeped her horn.

"Hi, Ernie!"

"Midge! Good to see you! What are you doing here?"

"I'm not working today."

"Can we go over to one of those benches on the other side of this walkway? I want to talk to you."

"OK. There's a parking area up ahead and some benches nearby. Follow me."

It had been over two years since they had seen each other. Ernie told her what had happened to him several months earlier with his job and he asked her if she knew of anyone who was hiring. She said she didn't, but she would ask a couple of her friends. He commented that it was great that she was driving and she told him that the car wasn't much, but it would get her around the area and she didn't need rides to and from work anymore. Then he asked her how married life was.

"Not good. I'm separated. I had a miscarriage last year and that caused lots of fights. I started crying a lot and I've been seeing Elaine at the clinic every week. Then I got colon cancer at the beginning of the year but I'm doing a lot better with that. I'm going for treatments but I think they caught it early. He said he couldn't afford to take care of me, so we separated in July."

"So the guy's a jerk. I'm sorry, Midge. I'll always care about you. I'm so glad I met you here."

"I know you care about me."

They talked for another 20 minutes. She said she was still working at the hotel as the assistant head of housekeeping, but her husband had quit his job and moved to Connecticut. Ernie asked if they could start seeing each other again, but she said not until the divorce was final (she had just filed for divorce last week and all she could afford was a legal aid lawyer), but they could call or even see each other once in a while at the clinic. They hugged each other and exchanged phone numbers and addresses. Ernie was on a high when he rode his bike home. "First good thing that's happened to me in the past six months," he thought.

He saw Stu and Jake a few days later, both of whom seemed to give him advice as to how to proceed with Midge. He called her a couple of times that week, but he didn't send her flowers or go over to her place and drop in unexpectedly. They agreed to meet in back of the clinic once a week where there was a bench and have coffee together for the rest of the fall. The only job offer that came his way was for working at Subway on Saturdays and Sundays, but he would make more money collecting unemployment.

Ernie's luck changed in November. A good friend of Jake's, Vern, who was also an AA member, owned a small three-story office building about a few blocks away from where Ernie lived downtown. One of Vern's security guards quit. Jake asked Ernie if he might be interested in working there "under the table."

Ernie said to Jake, "Yeah. I'll to talk to him about it. I know who he is, and I think he knows me from some of the meetings when I spoke."

Jake replied, "OK. I'll call him and let's see if he can come to the meeting at the church and the three of us can talk after the meeting."

Vern got to the meeting late, but after everyone left Jake called him over and introduced him to Ernie. Vern, a stout, deep-voiced man about in his early 60's, smiled and gave Ernie a handshake, saying, "Yeah, I know you. I saw you give a talk about yourself at a meeting a few years ago. Jake told me about the bad break you had when you got laid off your job months ago. I'm looking for someone who can fill in as kind of a security guard - night watchman type Friday, Saturday and Sunday nights 5 p.m. to midnight. It's kind of an easy job, a little boring, but there hasn't been a break-in attempt since the winter of '86, and that was at 2 a.m. You'd be sitting at a desk, or answering the phone. You can bring in a radio and there are a few magazines at the desk, but twice an hour, you'd walk around the building and the offices, checking to see if everything was in place, including the bathrooms and break rooms. If anything is suspicious inside or outside, you would call me, or call the police if you can't get a hold of me. I know you probably have trouble with stairs but we have an elevator. Cleaning staff is here until about 9 o'clock on Friday nights and some other cleaning people are here for a few hours on Saturday, and they leave at about 6 p.m. So, you will see some human beings. Sound like something you'd like to do?"

"Maybe. I'd like to see the building. What's the salary?"

"I can give you $8.50 an hour under the table, paid by my own personal check when you come in on the Friday after you worked the week before."

"That's more than you're getting from unemployment," Jake said.

Vern offered to drive him over to the building right then, and Ernie hopped into his car. Jake came along with them. When they got there, Vern introduced them to Al, the night watchman on duty then. He and Vern took Ernie and Jake all around the building, explaining to Ernie all of the responsibilities of the position – check the locks on the front and back doors, and for each suite of offices, bathrooms, break rooms.

Al said, "You have to bring your own food – you can use the microwave on the first-floor break room. There's a soda machine there, too."

Vern added, "Clean up after you eat or drink anything. You can smoke in the break room but please, no more than a couple of cigarettes a shift. Note in the log book at the desk in the lobby the times you started and completed your walk through and print any comments, if necessary."

The first floor housed a small accounting firm and Vern's office in the rear. The second floor consisted of a travel agency with five employees. On the third floor there was a computer repair shop that also sold used fax machines and printers. Al said that the only time the alarm ever went off on his shift in the year he worked there was on one winter night when a stray dog tried to force his way in, out back. Once a few months ago he had to call the police because a homeless couple were sleeping on the side of the building.

"Nothing else. It's an easy job. The cleaning people are nice. They go about their business and make small talk with you," he said.

They all thanked Al, and after they got in Vern's car, Vern asked, "What's the verdict, Ernie?"

"I'll do it. When do I start?"

"Friday at 5 p.m. be here. Dress casually, but neatly. I'll make you up an ID tag you'll have to wear at all times. And one last thing: If you ever are drinking or doing drugs, or even show up hung over, you are FIRED! A man named Darnell will come in and take your place midnight to 7 a.m. He's a black guy about your age – heavy set. I think you'll like him. He'll let you out the back door when your shift's over."

"What about where I put my bike?"

"Leave it inside the door out back. You won't be using it in the winter, anyway."

He drove Ernie home, and Ernie thanked him, as Vern said, "See you Friday. Thanks, Jake."

Ernie called Midge right away to tell her the good news. She was happy for him, but she said she couldn't talk long because she wasn't feeling well. She was going to bed early to save her strength for work the next day. But she did agree to meet him for Thanksgiving dinner the next Thursday that a church downtown was hosting.

Ernie's first weekend on the job went well. He brought a little portable radio with him and a paperback book, along with a sandwich. He thought, "This can get boring, but I need the money and I don't have to stand all the time. I could never sell shoes again or work as a cook more than a few hours at a time. My bones are aching more every year. I'm gonna turn 40 next year and already I feel like I'm about 60. But I still have to look for work if I want to keep collecting unemployment."

Thanksgiving with Midge was very nice. She said her husband's lawyer was dragging out the divorce. She wasn't feeling right physically most days and felt "wiped out" most of the time when she came home from work. She was starting to lose weight, too. Ernie said he really wanted to come over and help her out, but she declined his offer because her husband reportedly had some friends spying on her to see who else came into her place so he could claim that she was having an affair. They agreed to continue to call each other several times a week and see each other at the clinic most Thursday afternoons.

It was also a quiet holiday season for Ernie. December was a very cold and snowy. He still went to the clinic every other Thursday, but he was mainly going through the motions of therapy – he really went to spend a little time with Midge in person. He wasn't making as many AA meetings, but still kept in touch with Jake regularly. Every weekend he trudged through the snow and biting wind to show up at his job, but he enjoyed being there except for some boring stretch of hours. He got a scare one night when he slipped on a patch of ice underneath snow and grabbed onto a lamppost to prevent a bad fall, but he hurt his left shoulder. This tempted him to buy some booze, but he was paranoid of what might happen to him with the Tegretol. Instead, he loaded up on Aleve, Anacin and Ben Gay. He still could not find any full-time employment, or higher paying part-time work that would allow for his physical limitations. Ernie had enough money to pay rent and bills, and to buy food and cigarettes (a pack would last him about five days), but not much else, although he had some money in a savings account for an emergency. Jake went out of town with his wife for the Christmas holidays and Ernie couldn't see Midge, although he bought her a Christmas card and went to her house to put it through her mail slot, along with a small pair of earrings he bought. She called and thanked him, and said that she was going to spend Christmas with Florence (who was still her supervisor at work) and her family. He tried to call Mike, who he hadn't seen in a few years, but the person on the other end of the call said that Mike moved back with his family over on the seacoast last summer.

Ernie felt lonely. He went to church Christmas day, which he thought helped him a little. He also went to an AA meeting before he went into work on New Years' Eve. As a precaution, he asked Darnell, who came in 10 minutes late, if he could hang around for a few hours until 3 a.m. before he went home.

"Yeah. You can stay out here and pull up a chair, or you can chill out in the break room. But you ain't gettin' paid for any overtime."

"That's OK. Thanks. I don't want to be around any drunks on the way home."

"You don't want to go out partying when the celebration is at its best?"

"I can't. I'm in AA right now."

"I'm cool with that. When I make rounds, come out here at the desk, just in case anybody tries to get in here or if some fools are fightin' outside."

"I'll call a cab around 3 o'clock."

Ernie thought, "I hope the '90s are better than the '80s. But this decade was still better than what the '70s were, back in the bughouse."

Chapter 30:
THE NEW DECADE – OFF TO A BAD START

The cold northern New England winter did not bring a thaw. Intermittent snow and ice kept coming, and this hindered Ernie from looking for full-time work. At least he had a part-time job and he was able to pay his bills. He also had enough warm clothes and blankets. Other than going to work and to an AA meeting nearby, he spent his time watching TV and reading a few mystery books he picked up from the library downtown. He cancelled a couple of clinic appointments due to the weather. Midge and Jake had phone conversations with him a few times a week, but he had hardly any other human contacts, except when he went to the store or some brief small talk with a couple of cleaning crew members. Ernie was worried that Midge was complaining more about how sick she was feeling. She was worried that he was sounding depressed and urged him to call Stu ASAP and get a clinic appointment.

He told her, "OK, I'll talk to Stu, but Dr. Brennan left last month and I don't want to see any new psychiatrist there because she switched me to Carbamazepine (the generic form of Tegretol) and that was good because it might be dangerous if I drink with it, and it mellows out my moods a little bit, anyway. I'm feeling down right now, but I'm not suicidal or anything like that. I refuse to get on any kind of cocktail of meds like those people at the bughouse were. You and I know better than that. We've come this far. We'll be OK."

"That's good that you feel that way, Ernie, but I'm sick. Elaine's arranged for me to see a cancer doctor tomorrow. I might have to quit work next month."

"I got to come over and see you."

"No. Try to see Stu on Thursday and I'll see you afterwards at the clinic."

"Call me tomorrow night. I love you, Midge."

"I love you, too, Ernie."

Midge didn't call. Ernie tried to call, but he got no answer. He was able to get an appointment with Stu the next day, which was Thursday, February 1st. The session went well, and Stu suggested he come to group therapy on Tuesday night. Ernie didn't want to do this because most of the time he went to an AA meeting with Jake on Tuesdays. Stu suggested he call some people he hadn't seen in a long time to re-develop a friendship, if possible. Ernie said he'd try that, but told him about how when he tried to contact Mike, he had moved away.

"If we play, 'Why don't you…, Yes, but…,'you'll get nowhere. Ask yourself, 'What have I got to lose?'"

"I'll look through the phone book. It's hard for me to trust most of the people in AA unless they're already a sponsor for someone, but I might try that route."

Fortunately, it was a relatively warm day, and he saw Midge in the lobby of the clinic and they went out to the back of the clinic where the bench was. They hugged each other. She became tearful."

"Midge, what's wrong with your eyes? They look yellowish."

"The cancer came back. It's not in my colon, but it's in my liver now."

Ernie teared up and said, "Oh, hell. What's gonna happen to you now?"

"I don't know. I have to have an MRI, and probably cancer chemotherapy treatments. Maybe radiation."

"What's an MRI?"

"Like a CAT scan only better. They started using them on people for all kinds of illnesses and injuries in the past 10 years. I got to have this done right away. I'm scheduled for this at the hospital in two weeks."

"Does your husband know?"

"No, but he'll find out sooner or later. He's probably hoping I'll die." She started crying.

"This is terrible. I'd like to do something, but I feel helpless."

"We'll just keep calling each other. If I don't answer, I'm probably asleep. I got to tell Florence I'm gonna have to quit in a few weeks. I don't have much sick time left."

"I feel like getting drunk, but I can't even do that."

"That's the worst thing you could do. Call your AA guy. Call the crisis line if you have to. I have to go home."

They hugged each other and they went to their separate residences. Ernie went to AA meetings as often as he could and saw Stu at the clinic every week all through February. He gave halfhearted attempts to look for work once a week at places he knew wouldn't hire him, so he could keep his unemployment benefits. Midge said that the MRI showed evidence of the cancer in her liver spreading and she was starting chemotherapy treatments. She was told she wouldn't be able to take radiation treatments. Because of this, she had to quit her job and she couldn't talk for very long on the phone to Ernie. Ernie didn't call the crisis line, but he did talk to Jake for a half an hour or so, a couple of evenings. There was no one else except Stu that he wanted to contact. Florence was helping Midge as often as she could, and near the end of the month, Elaine said that starting March 1st, she would do outreach sessions with Midge. This upset Ernie because he couldn't see Midge at the clinic anymore. About a week after that, in a meeting with Midge, Florence, and her oncologist, Midge agreed to be in hospice care, and to "get her affairs in order." Midge had lost 20 pounds in the past 6 weeks and her belly had swollen up like a balloon. The end was near for her, and Ernie was going through stages of grief with Stu in their sessions. He had all he could do to drag himself to his weekend job and not go off his medication so he could get drunk. Ernie felt that his world was falling completely apart.

In mid-March, Ernie started going to Midge's house to see her a few times a week. She gave hospice workers permission for him to come over. The first time he came, on March 14th, Ernie thought Midge looked like a sick bird.

"Thanks for letting me come over to see you. Maybe you can beat this thing."

"It doesn't matter anymore. I'm in pain once in a while. I throw up sometimes. I try to sleep a lot if I can. I can't talk to people for very long."

"I'll always love you, Midge. I'll always care."

"I love you, too, Ernie. Hold my hand for a little while."

Ernie stayed for 15 more minutes and Midge told him that he should go, but to call her tonight. He kissed her and left. On St. Patrick's Day, he brought her a shamrock shake from Mc Donald's, thinking that she might be able to have some of it.

"That's sweet of you, Ernie, but I think if I tried to have some of it, I might throw up."

"Well, the thought was there," he said, sadly.

"You did that because I'm Irish. We had a few good St. Patrick's Days together. Promise me you won't go out drinking tonight."

"I won't, but I feel like it. It won't be to celebrate. I have to work tonight, anyway."

After a while, Ernie left and he asked Paula, the Hospice nurse, "Can she get any better?"

"Probably not. That's why we're here."

He tearfully asked, "How much time does she have left, then?"

"Maybe a few weeks. A month, at most, I'm afraid. She needs a miracle."

"I'll keep coming every few days. When I call her, she can't talk for any more than a minute."

Paula replied, "I think she'd like that. I don't know if you're religious or not, but all you can do is pray when you're not here."

Ernie went to work when he was scheduled and attended several AA meetings every week, but he couldn't stop thinking about Midge. At home, he couldn't eat much and had trouble sleeping. When he watched TV or tried to read, he was mostly gazing at the screen or merely looking at the pages in the book. Stu, who was very supportive, urged him to call the crisis line if he felt it was necessary. Ernie refused to see the psychiatrist at the clinic for a change in medication, but he insisted that he was not suicidal. When Jake checked in with him, he told Jake that he appreciated his support, but not to worry because, "I'm too depressed to drink. Just give me a ride to a meeting if the weather's bad."

On Sunday, the 26th, he went to see Midge and she seemed slightly more alert, smiling, and Ernie was able to stay for an hour. After he kissed her goodbye, he thought, "That's the best I've seen her in a few weeks. There's always hope. I'll be back on Wednesday."

On Monday he went to a late afternoon AA meeting with Jake and was invited to dinner at Jake's house. Ernie didn't get home until 9:30. He called Midge Tuesday night, but didn't get an answer. He went over to her house, but it was dark and the front door was locked. He called the local hospital, but they could not give him any information about Midge, or even if she were a patient there. He thought, "What the hell happened to her? Who knows?"

At 9 o'clock the next day he went to the clinic. Stu took the morning off, so he demanded to see Elaine, who said that she would see him right away.

"Ernie, please sit down. We tried to get a hold of you, but either the phone rang and rang or the line was busy. Midge had a bad night Sunday, and she was rushed to the hospital on Monday. She passed away later that afternoon. I am so sorry."

"What! Nobody told me! Why didn't somebody come over to my house? I was home most of the day yesterday!"

He broke down and cried for several minutes before he could say anything else as Elaine hugged and comforted him. He sobbed, "I never got a chance to say goodbye to her. I loved that woman and she loved me. Where is she now – in a morgue?"

"She's gonna be cremated. Her husband and some of his family made that decision. I am so sorry. Life isn't fair sometimes." Ernie got up and screamed, "Her so-called husband who didn't give a rat's ass about her! What a bunch of bullshit!"

He got up from his chair and threw it, knocking down some items from Elaine's desk and he stormed out of her office. On his way out of the clinic, he picked up a paperweight from the receptionist's desk and threw it against the ceiling. Ernie sped away on his bicycle and miraculously made it home without getting in an accident. He called Jake at his workplace and Jake said that he could only talk for a minute but pleaded with him not to drink, and go to a hospital if he needed. Ernie told him that if he did that, they'd send him back to the "bughouse," and he'd try to kill himself first. Jake told him to call the crisis line and go to any AA meeting as soon as possible. Ernie hung up, and paced around his apartment. He refused to answer his phone.

After an hour, he thought, "My life is ruined. I need a new start someplace else if I'm gonna stay alive. I got to get out of New England. He went to his bank and closed out his checking and savings accounts. He had a little over $1000 in cash. Ernie went home and packed his clothes and other things into a couple of old soft covered suitcases – one large and one small. He then called the electric company and the phone company to tell them to shut off services today. Ernie called his landlord and left a message for him, saying that he had to vacate his apartment tonight due to an emergency. He ate most of the food left in the house. Finally, just before 5 o'clock, he put on his overcoat, called a cab and when the driver arrived, he said, "Take me to the Greyhound Bus Station."

A NEW ADVENTURE

In the cab, it dawned on Ernie that to make connections for anywhere else out of New England, he'd have to go to Boston first. As soon as he got to the bus station, he got a one-way ticket to Boston – South Station. There was a bus leaving for Boston at 6 o'clock. He sat alone in a seat near the back. As the bus pulled away for the hour and 20-minute ride, he thought, "I want to get far, far away from here. Get a new life. Get a new start. Leave everything behind. I'm gonna turn 40 next week. Maybe go all the way to the west coast. Get a place to live and a job. I can afford to spend $500 to get me anywhere away from here. I might be able to survive for two or three weeks with the rest of the money I got. Maybe a big city would be better for me than some gossipy smaller place where everybody bad mouths everybody else – someplace where nobody knows me or anything about my past. I got enough meds for a couple of weeks. That should be enough." He got tearful as he started thinking about Midge. He decided that at some point he would write a letter to Jake after he got settled. Silently he promised himself that he wouldn't drink – he couldn't afford it anyway.

When he got to the bus terminal at South Station, he went up to the counter and asked, "Will $500 get me to San Francisco one way?"

"I'm pretty sure it will. Let me check the itinerary for you."

After a few minutes, the guy said, "I can get you there for $430, but you won't arrive there until Monday morning. You'd change buses 5 times, and you got a lot of layovers for a few hours each in New York, Pittsburgh, Indianapolis, St. Louis, Tulsa, Amarillo, Albuquerque, Phoenix, San Diego, and L.A."

Ernie didn't wait to hear anything else. He said, "I'll be back later."

He went over to the Amtrak South Station not far away, thinking, "A bus ride like that would be a pain in the ass. I doubt if I could stand it. Charlie told me I should ride the rails somewhere at least once in my life. That would probably be more comfortable than a bus."

He went to the Amtrak counter and asked the clerk, "How far can $500 get me on a one-way ticket to the west coast?"

The clerk said, after checking, "The best I can do for that price would be $475 to Denver - and that's a good deal. You have to change trains with a 4-hour layover in Chicago. The train doesn't leave until tomorrow at 1 o'clock, though."

Impulsively, Ernie replied, "Great. I'll take it. Can I stay here in the station?"

"Yeah, at your own risk. It'd be safer for you if you checked your bags at one of those lockers around the corner – don't lose the key. You don't want to go to a hotel?"

"No, I'll be OK here."

After Ernie paid for the ticket, the clerk gave him the itinerary and said, gesturing, "Go over there to that gate. They'll call 449, The Lake Shore Limited. Here's your assigned seat. You can store your bags on the train in the overhead rack or put one under the seat. It's 22 hours to Chicago. When you get to Union Station in Chicago, four hours later you'll be on Amtrak #5 - the California Zephyr train. It's on your ticket and the itinerary. Have a good trip."

Ernie bought the Boston Globe, a couple of magazines, got change to check his bags, and found a vacant place at the end of a bench. He slept intermittently through the evening and night, and fearing for his safety, he did not go out of the train station. A few people tried to make small talk with him, but he didn't want to engage in any conversation. In the morning he got a cup of coffee and an apple turnover, and waited until he heard the call for The Lake Shore Limited.

Ernie hopped on the train, and someone helped him put his suitcase up on the overhead rack, while he kept the smaller bag with him. Fortunately, nobody sat next to him for the entire journey to Chicago. The seat was a lot more comfortable than any bus he'd ever been on. There was a one-hour layover in Albany, and he got something to eat at the station. It was dark when he got back on the train, and he slept on and off through stops at Buffalo and Cleveland, thinking about Midge and all the significant people in his life who he had encountered over the past 11 years. Ernie woke up to face the new day at 6:15 a.m. when the train pulled into Toledo for another hour layover. He got coffee and a donut, used the rest room, and sauntered back to the train, which pulled into Union Station in Chicago at 10:15 a.m.

At about noon, when he was stretched out in a chair next to his bags, a lady about in her late 40's sat down next to him and, with a smile, asked him if was traveling to California.

"No, Denver," he replied, not even looking at her directly.

"Hey, that's where I'm headed, too. You have family there?"

Ernie was suddenly interested and replied, "No, I don't know anybody there. Is that where you live – in Denver?"

"Yes. Why are you going to Denver?"

"I came from New England. I had to get away. I'm not running from the law, or anything like that. It's a long story, but my girlfriend passed away on Monday and nobody told me. I just want to make a new start on life and taking a train from Boston – well, Denver was as much as I could afford without being flat broke. It's been a bad year so far."

Her name was Fran. She had just come from the funeral of one of her friends who lived in Chicago. She was making the round-trip journey by train because she spent a year in Europe teaching high school English as a civilian working for the U.S. Army in Bonn, and she loved taking trains in her spare time there when she travelled.

They talked at length. Ernie told Fran most of his life story, and she seemed very interested. However, instead of telling her that he was in a state hospital for many years, he related that he had a lot of "odd jobs" through the '70s, including making crates in a workshop, working in a hospital laundry, working in a bookbindery, working at a paint store, and stuffing envelopes. He said when he was 29, it dawned on him that he'd better be trained in some kind of occupation, so he learned to be a cook in a restaurant, although most of the places where he worked were diners serving breakfast and lunch. Then he told her about his experiences working at a radio station, selling shoes, as a night watchman, and at a front desk in a hotel. However, he went into more detail when he described the best job he ever had - at the Senior Center - but that he was laid off last summer and living on unemployment ever since.

"Your girlfriend who passed away – were you in a long-term relationship with her?"

"Off and on for 14 years. We never did get married. She was married to someone else for a few years. I don't want to talk about it right now," Ernie sobbed.

"I'm so sorry," Fran said, as she put her hand on his shoulder.

"What about you – you've lived in Denver all your life? Tell me about Denver – I bet the weather's just like New England."

Fran said that she had lived in the Denver area from the time she was a little girl, and was divorced with two adult sons who were living there. She taught English at a community college and was going to start again in the summer. Her long-time boyfriend was currently Director of a nursing home. Then she told Ernie all about Denver. She talked about attractions in and near downtown: The State House, The U.S. Mint, Mile High Stadium, McNichol Arena, Museum of Western Art, Kirkland Art Museum, Cooper Theatre, Celebrity Sports Center, and The Downtown Aquarium. She said that there was a Visitor Center not far from Union Station where he could get a map and lots of other information. Also, she said the weather was probably much like the ski areas of Vermont and New Hampshire, except that the air is thinner because of the altitude, and the humidity is a lot lower than anyplace on the east coast.

"Do they have a free clinic anywhere? I don't have any health insurance right now. I take medication for seizures."

"There are a couple of them downtown, I think. What happened to you that you have seizures?"

"I fell off a roof in my early 20s and got a head injury and my right foot and right leg were broken so bad I walk with a limp and I can't drive a car. At least I can ride a bike. I take stuff I can buy at a drug store for pain. I'm starting to get arthritis in a lot of places the older I get. First thing Monday morning I got to find out where the Social Services office is."

"That's Denver Human Services. Near Federal Boulevard. I don't know if you can walk it from Union Station. Where are you planning on staying?"

"Some hotel for a few days. That's the first reason why I need to get to a Social Services office."

It was soon time for them to board the train. With a stroke of good luck for Ernie, they both had aisle seats - across the aisle from one another. Fran seemed to feel sorry for Ernie and Ernie got the impression that Fran wanted to help him as much as she could. During the 22-hour ride, when they weren't taking naps, Ernie opened up to Fran about Midge. He also admitted that he was an AA member, but that he hadn't had a drink in a long time, and that he really can't drink with the seizure medication he was taking. He talked about Charlie and Jake and how they helped him navigate life through his 30s. He hoped that he would like Denver and that he could possibly get a job where he wouldn't have to be on his feet all day, a place to live that wasn't in an unsafe area, and make a few friends. Fran said that, from talking with him, she thought he could accomplish all those things, but moving someplace as a total stranger at 40 years old would be a big adjustment on his part.

On Saturday morning they pulled into Union Station in Denver and disembarked from the train. Fran's boyfriend, Mitch, met her and immediately she introduced Ernie to him. She told him that Ernie came to Denver to start a new life, not knowing anyone. Mitch shook Ernie's hand, welcomed him to Denver, and pointed Ernie in the direction of an Information Desk. After they all talked for a couple of minutes, Fran gave Ernie her phone number and said, "Call me Monday night and let me know how you're doing."

Mitch was surprised and said, "We can't take in a boarder."

Fran replied, "I know that. I'll tell you all about him in the car."

Mitch and Fran both wished him good luck as they left. Ernie thanked them both, "especially you, Fran for listening to me."

Since Ernie knew no hotel would check him into a room before 1 o'clock, he figured he had to stay at the station for a while. He checked his bags in a locker, got something to eat, talked with a lady at the Information desk briefly, and went outside to look around. He thought, "What a difference in the air here. Some of these people wearing cowboy hats and boots. This looks like a clean big city – way different than any place I've ever been. But I want to start a new life, so I guess this is it."

A few hours later he was trudging through the area with his bags, hoping he wouldn't get mugged or robbed. He checked into a cheap hotel and told the desk clerk that he would be staying for three nights, and checking out Tuesday morning. Ernie paid cash up front. The room was spartan-like, with a full-size bed, a desk, small old dresser, a clock radio, and a tiny bathroom with a shower. He unpacked, took a shower, took his medication, and went to bed. He was so exhausted from his journey that he slept right until about 5 a.m.

Sunday morning, he wrote out a step-by-step plan for himself. He would go to a Social Services office first to see what help they could offer. He would need a place to stay. He would have to get some source of income – preferably a job ASAP. Then he would have to find a free clinic where he could get his medication. He would need to go to an AA meeting and get a sponsor. Learning the bus system would be essential. Finding pay phones and getting change to carry around with him would be necessary. He had to find out where the dangerous parts of Denver were. Ernie decided to go over to the Visitor's Center to get a map and ask some questions about Denver. The man at the Visitor's Center was very helpful, and he spent about 10 minutes with Ernie instead of just giving him a map and shooing him away. On the way back to the hotel, he bought a copy of the Sunday edition of the Denver Post. He spent all afternoon reading the entire paper to get an idea of what was happening around Denver. More important for him, he paid particular attention to the ads to look for employment and a possible place to live, writing down names and phone numbers. Ernie had two copies of Alice's letter of recommendation, and although he didn't tell Fran, he was going to try to use Fran as a local reference if needed.

That evening, for about an hour or so, he hung out in the hotel lobby and talked with the evening shift desk clerk, Rob. Ernie told him about his experiences as a desk clerk a few years ago back in New England, and they swapped stories about guests and the operations of their hotels. The procedures of both hotels were remarkably similar. Ernie asked him about the possibility of working at the hotel.

Rob smiled and said, "You'd have to see Will (the manager) about that tomorrow, but I doubt if he'd hire any east coast stranger. I'll talk to him about it when I come on tomorrow and see what he says, but don't get your hopes up. He doesn't need anyone full time, for sure."

"I'd really like to talk to him."

"I'll tell him about you. It's gonna take you a while to get settled here. When you go to Social Services your chances of getting help from them are 50-50, and they are slow, grouchy people, from what I hear."

Rob was right. Ernie showed up at Social Services a little after 8 a.m. and as he started to tell the lady behind the desk his predicament, she cut him off and gave him forms to fill out to bring back to her when he was done. After he did this, she took the forms and bluntly told him that they deal with families first and to wait until he was called. At 10:30 he was called back to see a caseworker. He told her his story of how he arrived in Denver, and she told him that she would like to help him, but she couldn't see him until Thursday at 1:30 and gave him an appointment card. She advised him to stay at the Salvation Army shelter if he couldn't afford to stay at his hotel for the rest of the week, but to call her and tell her where he was staying. Ernie bit his tongue, thanked her quickly and limped out of there in an angry mood, thinking, "Why the hell did I ever come here?"

On the way back to the hotel he ran into beggars and a couple of people who tried to sell him drugs, but he shook them off and went to his room to get the information from yesterday's paper about potential jobs. He decided to do that first, and then look for a place to live on Tuesday, but he would tell them at the hotel that he would have to stay over for at least another day or two. Ernie went to Union Station to use one of the pay phones there. The first place he called already hired someone. He went to a nursing home, and even though he showed them Alice's letter of recommendation, the interviewer didn't seem to trust him, and even asked if he had AIDS. Ernie walked out the door without even completing the application. He made another phone call to a new heating and air conditioning office who indicated they wanted sales, advertising and phone soliciting people ASAP. He ambled over to a building on Larimer Street and was told to ask for Zach Morgan. As he got off the elevator for the 4th floor, he met Mr. Morgan right away – a young guy about in his late 20s who told him to sit down in the chair next to his desk. Ernie told him that he was very new in town, explained briefly why he came from New England, and he said that although most of his experience was as a cook and in a Senior Citizen Center, he did have sales experience selling shoes in 1983-84, and even some experience supervising people. He showed Zach Alice's letter.

"A glowing reference from back in the east coast. You got a resume with you, Ernie?"

"No, but I'll fill out an application and put down my work history for you."

"You have any references locally?"

"Fran Johnson. She's an English teacher at the community college here in Denver."

Zach smiled and said, "Yeah. I had her for English 101 there five or six years ago. Nice lady."

Ernie said, "I don't know much about heating and air conditioning, but I'm willing to learn."

Zach replied, "I need a few people to work the phones to contact businesses all over the region and get them on board with contracts for our services. I just hired a lady this morning, and I want two other people to start real soon. We're a new heating and A/C company that's just getting off the ground. The way this works is that we'd have you and a couple other people calling on executives from a list of companies and you'd read a standard one paragraph blurb describing our company and the services we offer. If they ask any questions about installation, price, etc., you'd tell them that we will send a sales representative over to talk to them and show them a video of our products. If they are interested, put them on hold and get one of our sales crew to talk to them. You may get a lot of people hanging up on you or calling you names and telling you not to call again. You will write down the company's response to every contact you call and turn in the sheet at the end of the work day. If you get an answering machine, keep giving the sales pitch and leave our number for them to call back. We're setting up cubicles right now for people to make the calls. Telephone soliciting can get boring and frustrating. Do you think you could handle it?"

"Yeah. I'm interested. What's the work hours and the salary?"

$11 an hour plus 2% bonus for any new customer contract. You'll be making a base of almost $20,000 a year and if the company takes off, and you're lucky, you might even be able to double that. You get 2 weeks off a year – use the days any way you want. You get 5 sick days paid a year, and 10 paid holidays a year off. You get health insurance, but it's pretty much a bare bones plan. The workday is 8:30 to 4:30, with a half hour off for lunch. You can take a break for coffee, or to use the snack machines a couple times a day. Dress is casual but neat – you can wear jeans and a sweatshirt or t-shirt on Fridays. You don't have to wear a tie. How does this sound to you?"

"Great. I'd be working with two other people and you'd be my supervisor?"

"That's right."

"When can I start?'

"Formally, you can start Monday, and paydays are the following Tuesdays – week to week. I want you to come in Friday afternoon at 1 o'clock for training – it'd be an all-afternoon thing, but I can't pay you for that time. Is that OK with you?"

"I'll be here."

"Fill out the application and the W-9 form, and I'll show you around."

Ernie met Sally, Zach's secretary/ receptionist, who told him that he'd probably need to learn to use a computer and fax machine if he didn't know how. He met a couple of the sales people and a few of the heating and air-conditioning installers. Everybody seemed friendly. Afterwards, he shook hands with Zach and said he'd be back on Friday. He felt like he was on "cloud 9" leaving there, but now he had to ask Will, the hotel manager, if he could stay there by way of a weekly rate for at least the rest of the month. Then he had to call Fran.

Will said to Ernie right away, "Rob told me you got front desk experience, but if you're looking for work here, I can't hire anybody until football season, and then only part-time on weekends. I'm talking about late August through early January."

"I just got a job today and I start on Friday, but I don't get paid for a week and a half. Can you give me a weekly rate to stay here?"

"You're supposed to check out tomorrow. I can do $200 a week payable in cash every Tuesday through the end of the month."

"I'll take that deal and I'll give you the first $200 tomorrow morning," Ernie replied, thinking, "He's got me by the balls." I got to get another place to live. I can only eat once a day for the next 10 days. I haven't had a cigarette since I left New Hampshire (he never did smoke more than 5 or 6 a day) – I'm quitting smoking for good."

He went back to his room and called Fran later at a pay phone in Union Station.

"Fran, this is Ernie. You told me to call you."

"Hi, Ernie. Are you surviving here so far?"

"The best news is that I got a job and I start Friday afternoon. My boss is a former student of yours. I used you as a reference."

"You did what? Ernie, I only knew you for 24 hours! Who is your boss and what kind of a job did you get?"

"His name is Zach Morgan. He's gonna train me to be a telephone solicitor for his new heating and air conditioning company. The office is not far from here."

"I remember Zach. He's a young wheeler-dealer type, so be careful. Did you go to Social Services?"

"Yeah. I got an appointment to see a caseworker on Thursday afternoon. These people aren't exactly friendly. Now that I got a job and I'll be getting paid in a couple weeks, I'll need help from them with a place to live, get set up with a free clinic for a little while so I can get my meds, get information about AA meetings, and where church suppers are. Life begins at 40. Today's my birthday."

"I remember you said that – happy birthday! I told Mitch and convinced him for us to take you out to dinner tomorrow night. Are you staying in a shelter?"

"No, I'm staying in a cheap old hotel up the street from Union Station. I'm gonna be there on a weekly rate until the end of the month. It's much like the place I worked at several years ago."

"We'll meet you at outside Union Station tomorrow at 5:30. There are a few nice restaurants in and around there, as you may have seen."

"Thanks, Fran. I'll be outside there."

The next morning Ernie paid Will $200 in cash for his weekly rent and called Alcoholics Anonymous. He found a meeting at noon about eight blocks away from his hotel. Fortunately, he was able to speak at the meeting. Afterwards, Ernie approached a guy about his age named Joe (he spoke first during the meeting) and asked if he would sponsor him. Joe, who came to meetings on his lunch hour a few times a week, said he would do this on a temporary basis until he got to know Ernie better. He told Ernie to call him a few times a week because he felt Ernie was very vulnerable at this time. There was one big link between Ernie and Joe - Joe was a fellow New Englander who had spent most of his life and career in Burlington, Vermont until promotions sent him to Minneapolis in 1986 and a year ago to Denver. They had a quick cup of coffee after the meeting, and Joe gave him his phone number. Ernie liked him right away.

Ernie went back to his room relieved that this was another piece of the puzzle put together in his life. He couldn't stop thinking about Midge, though, and he wished she could have been with him. He decided he probably needed to see a counselor, but that the big city of Denver wasn't as safe as anyplace in a small town in New England at night.

Later he met Fran and Mitch and they took him to a place called the Buckhorn Exchange. Ernie looked at the menu and saw Buffalo Sausage, Rocky Mountain Oysters, Rattlesnake, and Elk. He looked at them, shocked and said, "What the hell?"

They laughed and Mitch said, "Go ahead and order the New York Steak."

It was the best dinner Ernie ever had in his life. As he kept thanking them, Fran told him that she had another surprise for him.

"My aunt owns a house that was converted into several apartments about a mile away from the community college campus, and she has an efficiency apartment that will be available for rent on May 1st. It's in a good section of town, not far from a grocery store and Walmart."

"How much does she want for it?"

"$550 a month plus electricity."

Ernie, who was always good at math, calculated that he'd have just enough money to do it, and said, "Yeah, I'm definitely interested. Can I come out and see it this Saturday? Can I get a bus to get out there?"

"It's two blocks or so from a bus line that would take you back and forth from downtown near where you work and it's about a half hour ride, but call me Thursday night and I'll see if I can pick you up and bring you out there, if she's available."

"Thank you, thank you, thank you! You and Mitch have been wonderful to me. If there's anything I can ever do to help you, please let me know."

They drove Ernie back to his hotel when dinner was over. Ernie kept thinking that maybe Fran could turn into someone like the big sister he never had. The only social services help he needed now was to find a free clinic and maybe startup welfare money, as well as food stamps. He could not believe that things were falling into place for him so quickly. He never in his life had a streak of luck this good before. But he really felt sad that Midge couldn't be with him to enjoy this ride.

Chapter 32:
A YEAR IN DENVER

When Ernie went to his social services appointment, he was told that his caseworker was out sick and wouldn't be back until next week, and that if he needed help now, he'd have to fill out the same papers all over again. The lady at the desk said they may or may not get to him today. She asked if he had AIDS.

Ernie yelled, "No, I don't have AIDS! This is bullshit! Can anybody tell me where there's a free clinic I can go to because I'm running out of medication?"

An elderly man sitting on a bench nearby got up and told him where there was a free clinic but it would be a long walk. Ernie pulled out his map and went there. After another one hour wait, he was seen by a nurse practitioner who got him a one-month supply of Tegretol. That night when he called Fran, she said that her aunt, Martha, would like to meet him

Saturday morning at 11. Fran would pick him up out in front of Union Station at 10:30.

At his training session on Friday, Zach introduced Ernie to Jennifer and Lenny, who would be starting work with him as telephone solicitors on Monday. Zach gave each of them a sheet with large printed instructions on what to say to people taking their calls ("Smile when you dial," he said). He had them practice various scenarios and how to handle responses. Zach also showed them a sample of sheets with businesses and phone numbers to contact ("I expect you might have 50 or 60 calls to make a day"), and to submit each sheet to Sally when they were done. He showed them how to use the fax machine and the copier. Finally, he showed them their cubicles set several feet apart from each other ("Open desks would be too distracting"), and where supplies were (pens, pencils, note pads, etc.). They were "ready to roll" on Monday morning.

On Saturday, Fran drove him out to meet her aunt Martha and to see the apartment. Martha was a pleasant elderly lady in her 70s. The person living there (he was not home then) was to move out on the 28th, Martha said. She had heard about Ernie from Fran, and wished him luck in his new job. The apartment was on the first floor of a large house on a street corner. The unit was located in the rear of the building with a private entrance. It featured a spacious combination living room and bedroom area, a small kitchen, and a small bathroom with a shower. The unit would be partially furnished. A queen-sized mattress and box spring would be in place, as would be a Lazy-Boy recliner, a small kitchen table, a chair, an electric range and a refrigerator. The current tenant owned the rest of the furniture. There was a small backyard.

Ernie smiled as he saw the setup, and said, "I like it. Martha, I'll take it, but I can't pay you the rent until the day I move in – I 'll get paid on May 1st."

"I'll do that as a favor to Fran, but if you aren't here with the rent money by 6 o'clock that night, then it's no deal. I'll rent it to someone else.

Rent is month to month, payable on the first day of the month. You can have people over, but no parties of more than seven or eight people, and no loud TV or music after 11 p.m. You are responsible for keeping the apartment clean. There's a washer and a dryer in the basement that tenants can use. If any of the appliances or furniture get damaged not as a result of an accident, and if I find that there is any evidence of illegal drugs or other illegal activity, you'll be evicted right away. I don't live on the premises, but I will come over unannounced at least once a month during the week to check on the condition of the apartment. I'll put all this in writing and you will sign the agreement the day you move in. Is that acceptable to you?"

"That's a deal. I'll call you that day. I'll take off from work that day and the next day."

"There are stores and a Walmart only a couple of blocks away. The bus stop is two blocks away, too. I think buses run to downtown every 30 minutes – you can check that."

Fran said, "It's a nice, safe neighborhood. A good area to walk or ride a bike."

Ernie said, "I can't drive, but I can ride a bike and I hope to get one at some point. There are some other people who live here?"

"A young couple lives in the other apartment across the hall. Upstairs we have a middle-aged lady, and a single girl who works at the community college – Fran knows her."

"I want to live here. This is nicer than what I've been used to."

Martha said, "Good luck, Ernie. I'll hold the apartment for you until 6 p.m. on May 1st. If you can get here sooner that day, please call me."

"I will. Thanks, Martha."

Fran drove Ernie back downtown. He said, with a tear in his eye, "This will be the best place I ever lived in, in all my life. I'm worth it now. I just wish Midge could've been with me here."

Ernie told himself that he had to do as good a job as possible for Zach, no matter how frustrating work became. Hang-ups, insults, and other rejections over the phone brought him back to his days selling shoes and he kept telling himself not to take things personally. Lenny worked sales jobs before and he was a smooth talker. He told Ernie not to be discouraged if he came up empty most days – "It's like going fishing, or trying to pick up a chick at a bar." Jennifer could relate to some of the females over the phone and she tried to use her sexiest voice to help persuade some of the males. At the end of the first day, Lenny got three leads – one promising sale. Ernie got a lead from someone who wanted a representative to come over to discuss more information – Ernie successfully faxed his secretary the brochure. Jennifer came up empty. Zach was vague about what his expectations were from the three – he was starting to spend more time on radio, TV, and newspaper advertising.

Sales referrals for Ernie, Lenny, and Jennifer were few and far between most days during the first few weeks, and they were supportive of each other. But Zach was appreciative of leads and sales - "Turn it over to our sales people and they'll go in for the kill. Like the Godfather, we'll give 'em an offer they can't refuse. At least, most of the time."

Jennifer said, "Apparently, Zach felt that we're doing well – nobody's getting fired yet, in spite of all the rejections."

At the end of the month, Zach met with the trio and said, "You guys are doing OK – all of you are performing about the same. I was hoping we'd do even better, but looking at the statistics, the sales are about what most businesses get starting from cold calls like yours. Hang in there and don't let the frustration get to you. Just savor your part in any sales we get."

In the meantime, Ernie was surviving on a marginal existence, but he had been through this before – just in a different environment. He went to AA meetings, and he called Joe three times a week. Joe said he'd meet him for breakfast at the McDonald's downtown every Saturday until he got settled in his new apartment. He called Fran once a week. He opened up a checking account with a bank downtown on his lunch hour the day after he got his first paycheck. Lenny kept asking if he and Jennifer would go out to a happy hour on Friday afternoons, but every week they both told him they'd take a raincheck on that.

May 1st was another major life change for Ernie. Zach let him have 1 ½ days of personal time off to move out and get settled in his new place. Martha met him there, as he gave her the rent and she gave him the keys. It would take a few weeks for Ernie to buy new clothes and furnishings for the apartment, as well as a second-hand bike, and find a medical provider, but work kept going well right through June and he was established in a comfortable routine. The job was getting boring and frustrating at times, but the pay was great, he was becoming very skilled at his work (at one point, Zach told him that he hired him because of his "obvious survivor street smarts"), and he liked all of his co-workers.

One day in July, as Ernie was coming out of an AA meeting with a group of people downtown, Lenny was walking to his car after coming out of a bar another block away. Lenny called to him, but Ernie didn't see him, as he got into Joe's car - Joe drove Ernie home. The next day, as Lenny, Ernie and Jen were eating lunch, Lenny inquired about where Ernie had been after work.

"Ernie, did you come out of an AA meeting with those people yesterday? I called you and you didn't answer me."

Ernie brusquely responded, "What if it was?"

"So that's why you never wanted to go to happy hour with me. Are you a drunk?"

Ernie responded in an irritated tone, "Listen, Lenny, I have about 2 years of sobriety. You keep going to all these bars and happy hours and maybe you'll join us someday - if you want to."

Jen firmly said, "Lenny, I'm in Al-Anon. My mother is an alcoholic. Show some respect."

Lenny apologized, said he wouldn't tell Zach, and said, "Hey, we're still friends. Instead of a happy hour, maybe we can all go out to dinner some Friday after work. Or at least to get some ice cream."

Jen replied, "That's more like it."

Ernie said, "As long as it's not some bar."

By the time Ernie had been in Denver for several months, he had a support system – Fran, Mitch, Joe, Lenny, and Jen. At one time or another in August they all came over to his apartment at least once to hang out briefly (Jen brought her new boyfriend to meet Ernie). Ernie started to go to Mass most Sundays just to be around people, to thank God for keeping him alive, and also to light a candle for Midge. Fran wanted him to take a course at her community college. Ernie declined, but after he saw the continuing education catalog, he said he wouldn't be averse to taking a no-credit course a couple of nights a week for 5 weeks – History of 20th Century American Music. The course started on September 4th.

Life for Ernie, by that fall, was the most normal he had experienced in three years. There were times he was actively grieving over Midge, but he decided to work through it on his own rather to go into therapy again. Fran, Mitch, and Joe listened to him when feelings of sadness hit, but he called the local crisis line about every few weeks when he was feeling depressed over Midge. Joe became much like Jake back in New England. In fact, Joe took him to see the Denver Broncos play the Pittsburgh Steelers one Sunday at Mile High Stadium, which was a real treat for Ernie who had only been to high school games years ago. The Broncos lost but Ernie had a great time. He never dreamed that ten years ago he'd be at a pro game of any kind, and he thanked Joe for taking him.

During the course he took at the community college, he met a lady named Terry who sat next to him in the class. She was a secretary in the Business Department at the Community College. She knew who Fran was, but not personally. Terry laughed about his time at the radio station years before and was in awe of how he took off for Denver earlier in the year. She was about Ernie's height, fairly thin, in her late 30s and last year became divorced (no children) after a 10-year marriage. She told him, "The bastard was a drunk who started hitting me. I'll never get involved with anyone again who's a heavy drinker." At the end of the course, she asked Ernie what he did for fun lately (he had told her about Midge). When he replied, "Not much of anything," she gave him her phone number and said for him to call her when he was ready to go out and have a good time. Ernie thanked her and told her he'd "keep it in mind."

Ernie "kept it mind" for about two weeks and called Terry. She knew that he couldn't drive. She knew he walked with a limp, and she asked if he was wounded in Vietnam. He told her it was because he fell off a roof 20 years ago and damaged his right leg and foot, and he didn't want to talk about it because the injury made him feel defective, but at least nothing had to be amputated. He admitted to her that he was in AA and hadn't had a drink in 2 years and that now he couldn't drink anything because of the medication he was taking for seizures.

"Terry, you're not gonna hang up on me, are you?"

"No. I like you. Something about you – I feel sorry for you. I bet you had a rough life."

"Yeah, but things are better for me lately. Do you want to go out and see a movie somewhere this Saturday? I'd have to take a bus and meet you somewhere."

"I can pick you up wherever you live."

It turned out that Terry lived about five or six blocks away from him. They went to see a movie called "Reversal of Fortune," and both really enjoyed it. Ernie invited her in to his apartment afterwards "for coffee or a soda." She looked around once she got in, and said, "This is tiny. I have a better idea. Let's go to my place." Ernie wound up spending the night with her.

Ernie was on a high for the rest of the year. He was more energetic at work. Jen asked if he was in love. Lenny said, "Ooh – Ernie's got a girlfriend!" Zach was becoming more interested in radio and TV ads, and billboards, and his supervision of the three people who worked the phones became much less "hands-on," and he delegated some of this responsibility to Sally.

It was nice to have a girlfriend not far away for the winter, especially because in the cold, snow and ice he couldn't ride his bike over to see Terry. Ernie and Terry went to Fran and Mitch's for Thanksgiving dinner. They went to each other's office Christmas parties, and exchanged Christmas gifts at her apartment on Christmas Day. At times Ernie kept silently comparing Terry to Midge, but he tried to tell himself Midge was part of New England in his "rear view mirror," and this was one of the best periods of his life.

Terry went to Phoenix over the rest of the Christmas holidays to see her parents and other family members. Ernie was hoping to get invited, but he rationalized that they'd been going out for only 2 ½ months. When she came back in early January, they still dated, but Ernie sensed that the honeymoon period was fading away. At times they argued about whether or not Ernie could do more with his life, personally and occupationally. One night they had a loud verbal skirmish. Ernie became angry when she suggested that he might be using his physical handicap as an excuse to "stay in a dead-end job." He retorted that comments like that might've driven her ex-husband to drink. Terry told him to get out and walk home. He called Joe because he had the urge to drink. Joe came over and brought him to an AA meeting and spent about an hour at Ernie's apartment afterwards, which was very helpful to Ernie. Ernie and Terry made up and apologized to each other a couple days later. Terry said that her family wanted her to come home to Phoenix to live, and she told Ernie that she was considering moving there in the spring.

Ernie anxiously asked, "Are you breaking up with me?"

"No. In fact, you might even improve your life if you went to Phoenix, too. Seriously, how many years, or even how many more months will Zach keep you doing telephone soliciting. It sounds like his business has been taking off for the past six months. Do you think he'll promote you to a sales job? See what happens over the next month or two. From what I saw when I met your colleagues, Lenny seems ambitious and it seems like Jen is thinking the job is really a "job." You probably have one move left in your life in terms of any kind of a career. Once you get in your mid-40's you'll have age working against you."

"What the hell else can I do? I could work at a Senior Citizen Center again, but I can't be on my feet as some kind of cook all day. Arthritis is setting in more and more the older I get."

"You have to figure it out. I'll help you if I can."

Terry was right. By mid-March, Lenny was promoted to a sales job and Jen quit to work as a bank teller. Zach didn't fill their positions, and Ernie felt like he was getting swamped initially, but by April phone contacts were getting less and Zach wanted to cut Ernie down to half-time by May 15th. Terry told Ernie she was quitting her job and moving back to Phoenix. For about a week, he contemplated what to do, given that his situation was radically changing – phased out of his job and at a crossroads with his girl-friend. He talked to Fran, Mitch, and Joe and asked for their advice. They were supportive, but they understood his dilemma and it sounded like if he went to Phoenix, Terry could help him.

That Friday night, Ernie asked Terry, "Can I go with you to Phoenix?"

"Let me think it over. Let's talk Sunday afternoon."

Terry said "yes" on Sunday. They agreed to give their two-week notices to quit their jobs and to move out of their residences on April 30th. Terry was going to spend the next week in Phoenix, using leave time she was owed to find them a place to live.

On Monday, Zach wished Ernie well and said he would give him a letter of recommendation. Lenny took him out to dinner. Joe wished him luck and told him to go to an AA meeting once he got there. Fran and Mitch said they were sad to see him go, but to be sure to stay in touch. The year in Denver was over on April 30th for Ernie, as he and Terry loaded up her station wagon and drove to Phoenix to their new residence.

Chapter 33:
EPILOGUE

Terry found a job right away working as a secretary at a real estate company. Ernie was not so lucky. After being unemployed for two months, he and Terry started fighting over day-to-day living aspects – chores, staying in vs. going out, meals, and Ernie's unemployment (he was not willing to take a part-time job at a fast-food restaurant until something better came along). He got the impression her family members didn't like him. One night in July, in the midst of a confrontation, she said that her mother told her that she could "do a lot better" than him. Ernie retorted that Terry was not exactly the woman that Midge was. The next day Terry told Ernie that he should leave – "go back to Denver or the east coast, or someplace else. This isn't working for us together. Even if you got a job, I just think we're incompatible now."

Ernie when out to a nearby bar and got drunk. He was laughed out of the bar when he lost some money playing pool. When Terry came home from work she said, "That's it – I want you out of here tomorrow!" He was fortunate to get a room at the YMCA, and moved in temporarily. The next day, he was back in AA and soon found a sponsor, a guy named Mel. He never saw Terry again, and he never had a steady girlfriend again, either.

Several weeks later, he was hired to work 20 hours a week as an activities assistant at a Senior Services Center which paid $11 an hour, but with benefits. Two things helped him get the job: Alice's letter, and the Director's husband, who was in charge of financial services, had a relative who happened to be one of the regulars for the past 10 years at the same Senior Center where Ernie worked in New England. That person said, "Ernie was wonderful." Ernie's luck started changing. He moved into a small apartment within walking distance of his job in September. Mel helped him get some furniture and moved him into his new residence. He started making a few friends and found another part-time job, 2 days per week, working in sales at a ticket counter at a local theater. He also liked the Arizona climate, also. It was better for his arthritis.

Ernie lived in this routine – going to work, riding his bicycle, going to AA meetings, being in touch periodically with a few friends – for four years. His supervisor, Ellen, took a position as a Lifestyle Director at a new Senior Center in Mesa, and asked Ernie to be her assistant. This was a full-time position with excellent benefits. He'd be making about the same salary he was making in Denver, but the job would be less stressful, and he would have similar input into the programs of the Center as he had years before. He would even help out in the kitchen as needed. Ernie jumped at this offer and moved to Mesa.

Mesa wasn't very far from Phoenix, and he kept up with friends he made in his four years in Arizona. He found a new AA group and sponsor. He moved into a nice studio apartment in a big apartment building in Mesa. His new job was as good as what he had in New England, and he didn't have to work part-time to supplement his income. Overall, things were comfortable in Arizona for him, and this was one of the happiest periods of his life.

Five years later Ernie was in a bicycle accident when a car forced him off the road, blowing out his front tire, and he crashed into a pole. It took him a month to recover from his injuries, and when he went back to work, he struggled. On the advice of one of his friends, he eventually filed for Social Security Disability, and Ellen concurred with his decision to do this. He was awarded benefits and did not work again. He started using a cane, then gradually a walker, and by the time he was 55, he had an electric wheelchair. He started coming to the Senior Center as a participant in his late 50s.

Ernie never left Mesa. He never was admitted to any psychiatric facility again, but his physical health steadily declined and he passed away in September, 2022. He made peace with his mother before she passed away 10 years earlier, and also a long-lost brother who he contacted via the internet in the last year of his life. He never stopped thinking about Midge, and most likely, Ernie's last words were, "Where's Midge?"

About the Author:

P.J. Lamb is a retired psychologist living in Florida. His long career in mental health included 10 years working as a Chief Psychologist at a state hospital. He is a sports fan, enjoys 20th century music, walking on the beach at low tide, and he regularly posts various topics in alongtimeago.blog.

Previously published through Book Baby by P.J. Lamb: Taking The Local Train (2019).